Picture This

Second Edition

Photography Activities for
Early Childhood Learning

SUSAN ENTZ

CORWIN
A SAGE Company

For information:

Corwin
A SAGE Company
2455 Teller Road
Thousand Oaks, California 91320
(800) 233-9936
Fax: (800) 417-2466
www.corwinpress.com

SAGE Pvt. Ltd.
B 1/I 1 Mohan Cooperative
    Industrial Area
Mathura Road, New Delhi 110 044
India

SAGE Ltd.
1 Oliver's Yard
55 City Road
London, EC1Y 1SP
United Kingdom

SAGE Asia-Pacific Pte. Ltd.
33 Pekin Street #02–01
Far East Square
Singapore 048763

Printed in the United States of America
Library of Congress Cataloging-in-Publication Data

Entz, Susan.
Picture this : photography activities for early childhood learning/Susan Entz. — 2nd ed.
    p. cm.
Includes index.
ISBN 978-1-4129-7128-7 (cloth)
ISBN 978-1-4129-7129-4 (pbk.)
    1. Pictures in education. 2. Early childhood education—Activity programs. 3. Photography. I. Title.

LB1043.67.E58 2009
371.33′52—dc22   2008051641

This book is printed on acid-free paper.

09 10 11 12 13 10 9 8 7 6 5 4 3 2 1

Acquisitions Editor:	Jessica Allan
Editorial Assistant:	Joanna Coelho
Production Editor:	Veronica Stapleton
Copy Editor:	Gretchen Treadwell
Typesetter:	C&M Digitals (P) Ltd.
Proofreader:	Caryne Brown
Indexer:	Kathy Paparchontis
Cover Designer:	Michael Dubowe

Contents

What's New in This Edition?

The field of education continues to evolve, and this is especially true in the application of technology to curriculum and instruction. This edition features a section that summarizes the amazing advances in digital imagery that are now available to classroom teachers and care providers, along with three new chapters of sample lessons. One of the new chapters highlights the movement in early childhood education toward ongoing assessment, the adoption and use of standards, and systematic documentation. Since children are now exposed to technology from birth, another new chapter highlights some developmentally appropriate uses of photographs and scanned images with toddlers. Finally, with the current emphasis on including children with special needs with their peers, the third new chapter features a sampling of digital curricular activities to use with children with special needs.

The activity ideas presented in this edition are designed to provide teachers and care providers with a sample of possible uses of digital technology as an instructional tool for young children. It is hoped that early childhood professionals will use these samples to launch their own experimentation with creative uses of technology to enhance curriculum and instruction.

Ages and Stages

There were questions after the first edition about which activities were appropriate for various age groups. All of the activities in Chapters 1–8 were done successfully with preschool children in a four-year-old grouping. Most have also been presented with positive results with three-year-olds and early elementary students. The new toddler chapter, Chapter 11, adds examples of activities that utilize digital images appropriate for children fifteen months to three years of age. Some older children have also enjoyed these activities as a review. The ideas in Chapter 12 on children with special needs can be used with a wide age range, depending on the function level of each individual child.

Materials and Equipment

The materials needed to create the activities in this book are those now commonly found in early childhood education settings. In addition to the usual craft materials (scissors, glue, tape, marking pens, rulers, construction paper, poster board, etc.), only a basic computer setup is needed to make the curricular materials featured here. A computer, digital camera, printer, and the appropriate connective cords are all that are needed. Since digital images take up a significant amount of memory, it is useful to have additional hard-drive space available. Fortunately, the cost of even large amounts of memory for a backup is quite reasonable. A scanner is a nice device to add because it allows the teacher to save digital images of children's work and still let them take home their creations that day.

Technology (Chapter 1)

The section on technology describes some of the digital and communication advances most often used in the classroom. The techniques that are used in the activities in this book require only basic computer skills. A few of the newer technological advances described in the technology chapter require more investigation, but with a little time and practice they are all easily achievable by early childhood practitioners. Because advances in technology occur so rapidly, it is important for teachers to continue to explore and experiment with new equipment and software as it becomes available.

Note: While Chapters 3–12 are designed as guides for teachers to use digital technology with particular parts of the curriculum or particular student populations, Chapters 1 and 2 are to inform teachers on the wide array of tools they have now at their disposal. For this reason, Chapter 1 does not list specific activities but instead provides a more preliminary understanding for teachers.

Standards, Assessment, and Documentation (Chapter 2)

Assessment is at the heart of good teaching. The ability to observe students carefully as they are engaged in the process of acquiring new skills provides the critical information needed to adjust instruction in ways that will facilitate learning. The information gleaned from observation allows the teacher to gear materials and lessons so the children are able to consistently work in their individual *zones of proximal development* during direct instruction, while working in their independent learning ranges during center time and free play. Skilled observation and informal assessment are critical to the *assess-assist cycle* that helps children master new skills.

This chapter describes several types of educational standards and explores ways to use standards to organize systematic assessment, inform instruction, and document children's progress in an authentic and meaningful way. Like Chapter 1, this chapter is for teachers' own professional development, so while various skills are specified, there are no extension activities for the classroom or use at home as suggestions for parents to work on with their children.

Toddlers and Technology (Chapter 11)

Modern babies are exposed to technology from birth. It is not unusual to see infants mesmerized by mechanical toys and toddlers who know how to punch the keys on a television remote control before they can turn a doorknob. This edition features a chapter on activities designed specifically for toddlers and young three-year-olds. The activities focus on important skills and concepts to be acquired at this stage of development. When children see the photograph being taken and then printed, for example, they are able to make the important connection between the concrete three-dimensional world and the symbolic world of the two-dimensional image. A display and discussion of photographs of children exhibiting the emotions typical of toddlers (happy, sad, mad, fearful) is an effective way to introduce words for emotions and to talk about feelings. This chapter features language development activities and foundation skills for early literacy and mathematical thinking that can be fostered through digital images.

Children With Special Needs (Chapter 12)

The use of photographs with familiar objects, activities, and people is a particularly useful way to engage children with special needs. These images give the teacher a way to talk about things the child knows and to freeze events at a point in time in our otherwise a fast-paced world. Once captured, the digital images can help the child understand what occurred and to develop the communication and social skills needed to use the information effectively. Photographs also provide important visual cues on what will occur next and where objects belong. The pictures serve as a wonderful tool to develop vocabulary, promote basic mathematical concepts, and to focus on acceptable classroom behaviors. The activities in this chapter were selected for their usefulness in facilitating a successful classroom experience for young children with disabilities.

Communication with family members is always important, but it is crucial for children who have limited verbal skills, health issues, and other special needs. A communication log that shares photographs and information about events at home and school and that goes back and forth daily is a useful and often a much-appreciated method for interacting with parents.

Acknowledgments

Corwin gratefully acknowledges the following peer reviewers for their editorial insight and guidance:

Michelle Barnea
Early Childhood Consultant
Independent Consulting
Millburn, NJ

Karla Bronzynski
First Grade Teacher
Eldora-New Providence
Eldora, IA

Jack Fontanella
K–1 Teacher
Harborview School
Juneau, AK

Laura Gulledge, MEd
Media Studies Teacher, Benjamin Russell High School
Adjunct Instructor, Central Alabama Community College
Alexander City, AL

Nancy B. Hertzog
Associate Professor
Department of Special Education
University of Illinois at Urbana-Champaign
Champaign, IL

Julee Loorya
Elementary School Teacher
Birney Elementary School
Redondo Beach, CA

This edition of Picture This *is dedicated to the memory
of my dear friend, colleague, coauthor, and master teacher, Sheri Galarza.
Her teaching was a blessing to a generation of young children, to their families, and to the
teachers who had the privilege of working with her. Her death has been a loss to all who knew her
and to those interested in quality education. There isn't a day that I don't miss her profoundly.*

About the Author

Susan Entz is an Instructor of Early Childhood Education at Hawaii Community College; the Early Childhood Specialist for the Center for Research on Education, Diversity and Excellence (CREDE); a developmental specialist/special educator for an early intervention program; and a consultant to various programs, including the State of Hawaii Department of Education and Head Start. A graduate of the University of Michigan, she also holds a master's degree from Teachers College, Columbia University, and has completed advanced training at Harvard University. She is the author of more than fifty articles on classroom curriculum and effectiveness in teaching. She authored an integrated science-based curriculum for young children and coauthored a series of six children's books and a curriculum based on Hawaiian legends that stresses character development. Susan is also the recipient of the Hawaii State Teachers Association Friend of Youth Award and the Hawaii Association for the Education of Young Children Award for Professional Leadership and was recognized by the Hawaii State Senate for her distinguished work on behalf of children. Her current professional interests focus on teaching strategies that provide successful educational experiences for all children.

Introduction

Babies are not like us. They are not short adults.

Jean-Jacques Rousseau

Children are not miniature adults. They think and learn in ways that were once natural and familiar to grown-ups, but that may now seem quite foreign. Effective teachers and caregivers use tools and techniques that build on youngsters' natural curiosity and ways of learning, while at the same time reacquainting themselves with the wondrous ways young children look at the world.

Picture This: Photography Activities for Early Childhood Learning is designed to introduce teachers to one such technique: the use of digital images in the classroom. The digital camera, instant photography, a scanner, a printer, and the computer are new teaching tools that can be used to create curriculum that capitalizes on the way young children learn, provides a simple way to document that learning, and shares that information with parents and other professionals.

Young children are egocentric learners

Toddlers, preschoolers, and early elementary school students are remarkably egocentric. The young child is truly the center of his or her own universe. Curricula must capitalize on the fact that young children are self-centered and self-absorbed.

Photography is a useful tool for teachers of young children. It puts the children right where they want to be, at the center of the action. Photographs of the children or taken by the children literally put them and their work into the learning activity. Children are encouraged, then, to explore areas of learning that are of vital interest to them and to create a visual record of the activities. Inviting children to select the pictures to be taken underscores the importance of their ideas and fosters creativity.

Young children need and want adult attention. The term "group" usually refers to the whole class, and the activities in this book can be introduced to the entire class. When dealing with very young children, however, a smaller group introduction is preferable. Each activity in this book also provides small-group tasks, one-on-one encounters, and follow-up ideas for parents.

Young children learn through play

The value of play is one area that truly separates children and adults. Recreation is what adults do when their more important work is finished or when they have nothing better to occupy their time. Play to young children is something quite different; it is a primary focus of life. It is the process by which they explore the world, interact with people and materials, and learn about who they are and what they can do. Play is the work of childhood.

Infants learn how to explore their world through play: by shaking a rattle, looking at a mobile, reaching out to squeeze Grandpa's nose, and via a host of other sensory and motor experiences. Toddlers are motivated to become mobile, in part, to reach toys or play partners. Preschoolers expand their social and emotional horizons to play cooperatively with other children. Kindergartners and first graders incorporate mathematics, literacy, and problem-solving skills into their play themes.

Through play, children work out problems or conflicts. They assume roles and say words that may not be safely expressed in real life. Children direct their own play, selecting activities and themes that are meaningful to them. Dramatic play allows youngsters to revisit real-life experiences, represent their understanding of how the world works, and develop their imaginations through fantasy.

Most important of all, play is fun. Children spend extended time in play because it is self-motivating. They get what they need out of their various play experiences.

Digital and instant photography allows the teacher to capture learning as it occurs. The activities described in this book involve children actively in the process of learning. Although each activity represents serious learning, it is presented playfully, as a "playjob" or something fun for a group to do together.

Young children learn to think

A young child's cognitive structures are different from those of an adult. The only way to get information from the outside world into a child's developing brain, where it can be understood and then remembered, is through the five senses and movement. Young children learn by doing. The younger the child, the more direct the learning must be. Being told about a chick is quite different from holding the chick itself, feeling its fluffy down, listening to its little peeping sound, and feeling it peck a finger. Personal involvement with people and materials is crucial for youngsters because they need to explore the world directly with their senses and muscles.

Adults can help children discover how the world works by providing a variety of firsthand experiences, being there to support this learning, supplying resources, and answering questions. Once a child has had a firsthand experience, she or he has a mental picture of it and can draw on that mental picture in the future. Teachers facilitate learning when they provide a scaffold to help children move from simple to complex, from concrete to abstract thoughts. Quality instruction helps children recall what they already know and build upon that knowledge to go to a new level of understanding.

Digital and instant photography helps young children to revisit their firsthand experiences shortly after they occur and to fix them in time. Pictures stimulate the recall of direct experiences, and the use of words as memory triggers to recall these concrete events.

Photographs taken during school events have the added benefit of extending school learning into the home. Pictures and photo-based activities can be sent home for the child to share with family members. These extensions offer the opportunity for additional practice, improved comprehension and recall, as well as language development. They also allow parents to know more about their child's school day.

Young children develop language

An explosion of language occurs during the early childhood years of birth through age 8 years. The development of listening skills, receptive language, and expressive language is vital during this critical period.

Children benefit from conversation about meaningful experiences in which they are engaged. They need ample time to talk and to be heard, to listen to language as it is spoken correctly, and to develop vocabulary. An adult's skillful and timely questions encourage discussion and have a positive effect on children's vocabulary and comprehension.

The activities described in this book put children into the center of the action. By their nature, these multisensory activities stimulate language and encourage self-expression. Photographs also bring past experiences into the present for discussion. The hands-on materials featured throughout this book encourage language development because they are meaningful to children and invite them to select and engage with the materials, and interact with other children and adults.

Young children learn holistically

Young children learn best when information is presented to them in context, where relationships and connections are made clear. Material that is presented in an integrated way is remembered more easily.

The activities in this book were selected to show a wide range of possibilities available to the classroom teacher. We hope they will be integrated into existing themes or units and serve as a springboard for future investigations.

Young children welcome new technology

Unlike many adults, young children are not technology phobic. In fact, they often embrace new technology. They can't imagine a world without microwave ovens or remote controls for televisions. Rather than seeing new tools as threatening or overwhelming, young children are challenged to see what they can make these gadgets do. In fact, youngsters may suggest using the digital camera and computer images in ways that teachers have not yet identified.

Whenever possible, children should be involved in the actual process of taking pictures. This should be done under supervision and only by those mature enough to understand the responsibility. The sooner they begin to "frame" pictures in their minds, the better they will become at finding meaningful images to capture on disc or film. Teachers may soon see an increase in the creative uses of these photographs.

Digital photographs taken either of or by the child encourage further exploration of the computer. Once the digital image is entered into the computer, it can be combined with other graphics or described in a written narrative. Children delight in being involved in these sophisticated skills and the hard copy their efforts produce.

Photographs provide feedback

Effective communication is a cornerstone of any successful venture. Photographs stimulate conversations between all key players in a school. Pictures provide feedback to children, to their parents, for reporting progress, and for staff development.

Digital and instant photography is a natural tool for use with young children because it provides instant feedback. The immediacy of the result provides very positive reinforcement for young children and encouragement to experiment anew.

One way the teacher can use the photographs is to spend a few moments at the end of each day with the children, looking at key pictures taken that day. They can talk about what occurred, the new things learned, the favorite activities revisited, and the human interactions captured on film or disc. Feedback is important for children. These chats give the teacher an opportunity to note progress or to share a word of encouragement to individuals or to the entire group.

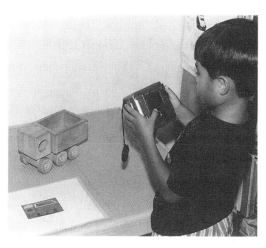

Young children are notoriously poor reporters about their daily activities. Photographs of the children engaged in that day's events provide one method for sharing information with parents. A few of the pictures posted in the sign-out area will give parents an idea of what occurred in class that day. The digitized photographs can be used again in the school newsletter to put activities into context and thus highlight areas of strength for the school. Photographs may also be added to a class photograph album, with a simple description of events placed into plastic page protectors and shared with family or visitors.

Representative photographs can be saved for the child's portfolio. A folder can be labeled with the key areas or domains to be examined. Throughout the year, the teacher can print and label pictures that depict the child engaged in one of these areas and that represent either growth or mastery of that subject. Photographs may also capture a child engaging in a preferred learning style. Teachers can use the checklists provided at the end of each chapter to document each child's progress and add to the portfolio.

Photographs enhance staff development

One benefit of documenting children's progress through photography is improved staff development. As teachers or aides look for proof that a child is working on a new skill or has mastered one, they are furthering their own evaluation skills. They first need to observe the child carefully and then interpret what they see, using their understanding of normal development in the different learning domains. This process sharpens their observation skills, improves their ability to interpret the meaning of what they see, and helps them identify these snippets of behavior as signs of growth and development.

When programs use a formal evaluation system of developmental scales, the teacher needs to understand each skill listed. Proof of this understanding is demonstrated by the activities he or she chooses to record on film. The picture not only shows the child's progress but also documents the teacher's ability to apply the evaluation format to the ongoing rhythms of a busy classroom. This type of documentation is sometimes referred to as "authentic" because it evolves from the child's own learning.

Using photographs to supplement an evaluation system prompts staff members to look at each area of the curriculum. Because the teacher needs to report on each domain, there is a greater probability that she will not be ignoring one or more important areas of learning. As the staff member becomes more familiar with the system of evaluation, she will develop a mental checklist that she will carry with her even when not involved in classroom photography.

As the teacher looks through the lens of the camera at a child, she is watching and listening more closely than she may be at any other time. She may discover things she had not previously noticed. Is the child exhibiting behaviors that may indicate a "red flag" for developmental delays? Has this child made a developmental leap previously overlooked?

Photographs taken for other purposes can be used for problem solving by the staff. They can share a photograph with the group and probe their understanding of what is going on. They can consider whether what is pictured is developmentally appropriate for children of this age. What does the picture say about the teacher's preparation of this activity or classroom management at this time? Photographs invite discussion about other ways the situation could have been handled.

Photographs are also quite useful for the self-study phase of program accreditation. Occasionally, the validator will not see an element that is on the evaluation form, but photographs serve as evidence that it does occur.

Finally, the use of photographs can turn periodic staff evaluations into a more reflective, self-evaluative process. Some staff members may even want to create their own professional portfolios. The digitized images taken to demonstrate a child's current level of motor or social development can also be used to show a facet of the teacher's skill. The photographs can document a broad representation of the teacher's work.

Using digital and instant photography has advantages

Digital and instant photography is an effective learning tool for a host of reasons. It is easy to use and encourages creative curriculum development, involves children actively in their own learning, captures them as they are engaged in tasks, and stimulates cooperative social interaction in the group.

Once the computer, printer, and digital camera have been purchased, digital photography is cost-effective. Teachers have the benefits of the pictures without the costs of film purchase and processing. They are also able to avoid the after-school commitment of time needed to drop off the film and pick up the pictures.

One digitized photograph can be used in a variety of ways and in a variety of formats. Multiple copies can be made of projects so that each child is able to take home pictures for extension activities.

Perhaps most important, a photograph of any individual grabs his attention and is motivating. Curriculum that involves and includes a child's own images holds his attention longer than other curricula do. It says to the child and his parents alike that he is a very important member of this class and that we are glad he is here.

1

Technology

TECHNOLOGY INTRODUCTION

When my dear friend, Sheri Galarza, and I wrote the first edition of *Picture This,* the educational use of technology in the classroom was in its infancy. There were, in fact, only three digital cameras available on the market and they were quite expensive. However, we recognized immediately the educational advantages of using pictures of the children, their activities, and the objects they used to enhance our teaching. Neither of us imagined the explosion in technology that would occur in a few short years. When the book was first published, we gave workshops to show teachers their first glimpses of a digital camera. Now, technology is so pervasive that preschoolers use discarded cell phones and second-generation digital cameras as part of their imaginative pretend play.

What is the educational policy on technology?

As access to computers, educational software, and other forms of digital technology has proliferated, educators have had to evaluate the role of technology in the lives of young children. Researchers have endeavored to identify the benefits and potential hazards of early exposure of young children to technology. Subsequently, professional organizations have developed position statements on the topic. The initial paragraph of the white paper prepared by the National Association for the Education of Young Children (NAEYC), titled "Technology and Young Children—Ages 3 through 9," adopted April 1996 and modified in 2004, frames the topic appropriately for teachers and caregivers (to view in full, visit the NAEYC Web site at http://www.naeyc.org/about/positions.asp

> Technology plays a significant role in all aspects of American life today, and this role will only increase . . . in the future. . . . As technology becomes easier to use and early childhood software proliferates, young children's use of technology becomes more widespread. Therefore, early childhood educators have a responsibility to critically examine the impact of technology on children and be prepared to use technology to benefit children.

How can technology be used as a teaching tool?

Teachers have become "wired." As technology has become part of everyday life, educators have explored ways to include it in the classroom. What began as a novel add-on to the traditional curriculum has now become an integral part of the classroom. Teachers have experimented with ways to use the computer, and many of the new technologies have become vital teaching tools.

Professional organizations offer information for teachers on the uses of technology on their Web sites and in publications. When one enters the word "technology" into the search box on the National Association for the Education of Young Children Web site (http://www.naeyc.org), for example, a variety of references on technology appear, including a very useful list entitled "Links to Online Resources on Technology as a Learning Tool."

The Computer

In the past decade, engineers have continued to make computer chips faster and their storage capacity vastly greater. Memory sticks that are the size of a piece of gum have more digital memory than many of the computers used to send men to the moon. Access has continued to improve as schools and government agencies have made a commitment to putting computers into classrooms and public libraries. Commonly used computer programs are increasingly more user-friendly and varied in their function than their earlier versions. Software designers have realized the marketing potential for providing educational and gaming software that focuses on young children.

The Internet

What once seemed to be an overly ambitious title has become a reality; we truly have a World Wide Web. This amazing communications vehicle provides classroom teachers with unprecedented access to information and opportunities to share information with colleagues and with students' families. It's now possible to "google," meaning to search electronically, for information from the basic to the most exotic. High-speed connections have made the transmission of digital still images instantaneous, and digital video is now a common feature of many Internet sites. In fact, real estate agents offer virtual tours of prospective properties, and news agencies broadcast video clips of breaking news events on their Web sites.

Digital Cameras

There has been a technological shift in photography from film-based cameras to digital. Fortunately, while the physical size, memory capacity, ease of use, and lens quality of digital cameras have improved, the cost has come down. The result has been a proliferation in the use and availability of digital cameras. There are even models made specifically for children and plastic toy versions for dramatic play. Digital photography is particularly useful for capturing children's work in process-oriented activities, such as block building or water play. The materials will be put away at the end of the session, but the photographic image has frozen that moment in time for future reference.

Electronic Picture Frame

A nice way to feature classroom happenings is to take random photographs during the day and download them into an electronic picture frame before parents pick up their children at the end of the school day. The frame can be placed next to the sign-out sheet to give the parents a quick overview of the day's activities. Parents can then be encouraged to ask their child about the pictures,  recalling what happened during the day as a way to encourage conversation and facilitate both memory and vocabulary development.

Camera Phones

Even a decade ago, few would have imagined that much of the population, including schoolchildren, would be carrying mobile telephones. Some phones have features that allow the user to not only make calls but also connect to the Internet, check e-mail, and serve as a notepad, address book, clock, calculator, and day planner. This amazing little device may even have a map feature and voice mail. Had we been told before the turn of the millennium that we could use wireless telephones that would also take digital photographs, play music, send instant messages, and play digital videos we would have scarcely believed it. Amazingly, all of these things are possible today in an object the size of a deck of cards.

Photo Software

Paralleling the popularity of the digital camera has been software development that allows the home user and the professional to manipulate the digital images to create the desired effect. Rather than waiting days to send out film to be processed, the user can take a photo and have it downloaded, sized, edited, and printed in minutes. Even novices can experiment with their unexplored talents as a graphic designer.

Printers

Printer quality has continued to improve as the cost of the printer has come down. Most early childhood classrooms can now afford a color

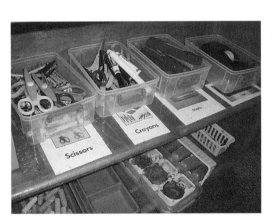

printer, and some clever teachers include color print cartridges on their school supply and classroom wish lists. The ability to print images immediately is a particularly valuable aspect of the use of new technology with young children, who respond so positively to the immediacy of the feedback it provides. Images of classroom materials and activities can be printed quickly and used to reinforce learning or provide visual cues to classroom rules and routines.

Screen Savers

A simple way to stimulate conversation and encourage recall is to use photographs of class events as the screen saver for the classroom computer. As children notice the images changing, encourage them to label what is seen and to recall what was happening in the class when the photograph was taken.

Scanned Images

The digital scanner is a useful classroom tool for archiving information for later use. When a young child wants to take home artwork, for example, and the teacher needs to retain a copy for the portfolio, both needs can be accommodated by scanning the drawing or painting before the child departs with her picture. The digital image can then be used in a variety of ways.

Clip Art

An array of free and low-cost clip art is available for download from Web sites. For example, the Microsoft site has 150,000 pieces of clip art, photographs, animations, and sounds for free download. Programs such as Art Explosion from Nova Development provide hundreds of thousands of royalty-free illustrations and photographs in all popular file formats for a modest cost.

Presentation Software

Digital images can be imported into presentation software, such as PowerPoint, to highlight instructional concepts, to prepare for parent presentations, or to create integrated individualized portfolios for each child that highlight progress over the school year. Presentations can also be created for training purposes or to share teaching techniques with colleagues.

Once the teacher or caregiver has chosen the initial design for the presentation, students can be included in its preparation. Even young children enjoy being asked to participate in the selection of photographs for a parent night presentation or to provide a quotation for a picture caption.

Publication Software

Digital images greatly enhance the appeal and visual presentation of publications. Formatted publications can be downloaded for software, such as Microsoft Word, to create classroom newsletters, fliers, brochures, invitations, calendars, and note cards. Templates can also be downloaded from the Microsoft site. Once the format has been selected, children can assist with the creation of publications by helping to select the photographs to be used and decide on their placement in the documents.

E-Mail

The increased need for communication appears to have grown with the number of ways to communicate. A photograph that depicts new learning or a special event with a brief note is a thoughtful way to keep parents informed about their child's progress.

A quick and effective way to keep families informed about current classroom events is through quick group e-mail. The few minutes it takes to jot down a brief description of class highlights, or to import a photograph, is rewarded tenfold with the trust it builds with the families that receive these daily missives from school. The same information and images can be printed and displayed in the classroom for family members who pick up their children to view.

Electronic Newsletters

Classroom newsletters are a wonderful way to engage the students and communicate with families, but they are time-consuming to produce and

the "news" is often outdated when it is finally delivered. An electronic version of the traditional newsletter is an effective way to provide timely information, highlight upcoming events, celebrate progress, and underscore ways that parents can support their children's learning at home. One technique is to set up a group distribution in a word-processing program with the e-mail addresses of all family members wishing to receive an e-newsletter as an attachment. Once formatted, the master can be used for all future editions. Relevant pictures or graphics can be inserted and text descriptors added before sending the newsletter as an attachment. The electronic version can also be printed and stored in a binder to display at parents' night or shared with the families of prospective students.

Digital Video

Video cameras have been popular for decades, but the shift to digital videos has transformed the medium. Parents and teachers can shoot video, edit the footage, and display it quickly on their computer screens, on their televisions, on large screens via an LCD projector, or shared via the Internet. The ability to capture the buzz of a busy classroom in action presents a treasure trove of possibilities for the creative teacher. Digital video footage is particularly useful as a tool to help children become more aware of the sequence of activities, their own behavior, and varying approaches to negotiation and problem solving. It is also of incomparable value as a tool

Happy Hands Playgroup News

Reading Is Fundamental Distribution

The March socialization group was a grand success. Children and parents gathered in the conference room for free play. During group time, the children learned the rhyme "Teddy Bear, Teddy Bear, Turn Around" and then practiced with their own bears. They had a chance to make a teddy bear hand puppet and join the teddy beartea party. Before going home, each child was able to select a new book compliments of Reading Is Fundamental.

Page 1 of 4

for sharing information with parents. Teacher training, reflective supervision, and staff development are also enhanced when footage of actual classroom events can be analyzed to inform future practices.

An additional feature of most digital video cameras is the capacity to take still shots and to create still frames that can be printed as individual photographs from a video recording.

Video Software

Advances in software have made it possible for a novice to import digital video recordings into an editing program to produce a movie, complete with voice-overs and a music track. Once finalized, the movie can be exported back to the video camera, transferred to VHS videotape, or burned as a DVD. These mini-movies are useful in a variety of ways, from documenting ongoing classroom projects to noting individual student progress over time.

Classroom Webcams

A webcam (Web camera) is a small camera built into, or connected to, a computer, which enables the user to send selected digital images or continuous live streaming audio and video via the Internet. This technology is used to monitor everything from daily traffic and the weather to real-time activities in the classroom.

Technology now allows family members to watch their children painting at the easel or building skyscrapers with wooden blocks, by way of a webcam transmitting from the classroom to a parent's computer at work or to grandma's house far away. Authorized family or friends need only to log on any time to a secure site to see what the class is doing and how their child is fairing at any given time. While initially intimidating, this technology has the potential to demystify parents as to what happens during the school day and to facilitate communication between home and school.

Student Videoconferencing

All computer users today, even young children, have the greatest access in history to people, places, and events separated by time and distance. Videoconferencing is a technique for connecting students in separate classrooms or school. It requires a webcam connection at each location for the students in remote locations to be connected. Students talk and share projects, questions, and ideas through the webcam that sends their input electronically to a distant location. By setting up a sister class relationship with a school in another location, students can learn about other places, cultures, and activities. For example, children in Hawaii can talk to students in Alaska via a computer videoconference. Before the hookup is established, the teacher facilitates the interaction by helping the children think of questions the group would like to ask their distant friends and information they would like to share about their own lives and interests.

The Virtual Classroom

Children with illness or disabilities that require frequent or prolonged absences from school can stay connected to the classroom via computer. Videoconferencing technology has made it possible for many hospitalized and homebound children to stay connected to their classmates and teacher during part of the school day. A webcam with a microphone is connected to a computer and an Internet connection in both the classroom and in the home or hospital room, allowing back-and-forth communication in real time.

Teacher Videoconferencing

Thanks to technology, the world has gotten smaller. Teachers from distant locations can meet and talk in cyberspace on topics of mutual interest via videoconferencing. One-on-one videoconferencing capabilities over the Internet use webcam technology and can be quite useful to share information and demonstrate techniques with colleagues. Programs such as Windows Live Messenger and iChat offer teachers a virtual meeting place where people can see each other and talk in real time.

Teacher Chats

Teachers from distant locations can share interests and concerns informally with others doing similar work by joining an education-based chat room. A teacher might post a question, for example, about curriculum or a problem she is having with her class and check for written responses from others in an online community who might have suggestions. Homecare providers are able to use chats to communicate electronically with others doing similar work about the unique challenges they face with their particular population. Instructions and graphics for projects also can be shared with colleagues through chats.

Internet Teacher Training

As advances in technology have occurred and teacher trainers have become more comfortable with its uses, more coursework has come online. Many degree programs in education offer courses online, and several programs are designed to utilize online learning for major portions of their training design. Hundreds of sites now offer sample lesson plans and curriculum ideas for classroom teachers. Information is now just a keystroke away. Sites such as TeacherTube.com offer an online site for teachers to locate and share instructional videos.

Class Web Site

One effective way to communicate with families and at the same time introduce young children to technology is to create and use a classroom Web site. It is a useful tool for sharing news or exciting classroom activities and for providing reminders of upcoming events. Some sites are easy to set up and are hosted for free by commercial sites, such as Scholastic.com.

Blogs

A blog (Web log) may be an alterative for educators who are not comfortable with the technology or ready to commit yet to a full Web site. Blogs are easy to set up and use. Some sites, such as edublog.org, are designed specifically for teachers. Blogs began as digital diaries with the latest entries displayed first but now typically include commentary on a particular subject. They can combine text, photographs, clip art and video, podcasts and audio, as well as links to other sites. Blogs can be set up so that family members can leave a message or respond to the teacher's entries.

Another method of creating an electronic newsletter is to set up a blog, featuring classroom events, and then send it via e-mail to families with the blog link.

iPods

The iPod (referring to "portable on demand") and other MP3 players began as portable music players. They are now being used for teaching and learning. These devices are a convenient way to store music or audio material to use in the classroom. Teachers can download the songs they want to use at circle time, for example, from various CDs or a source such as the iTunes store and arrange them in the order to be played. The ability to order the materials digitally before class eliminates the problem of losing the children's attention while the teacher searches for a desired song. The iPod is also a useful storage device for pictures, projects, and video work in progress; and because it is so portable, the material can be downloaded and worked on from various computers.

Podcasts

Podcasts are collections of digital media files that are distributed over the Internet and can be downloaded to the computer or iPod to be heard or viewed. The educational uses of this technology have increased as the number and variety of downloadable audio and video files have proliferated. Teachers can download audio or video files to bring information into the classroom via a podcast. They are also creating their own multimedia podcast presentations to emphasize classroom content or other information. That information can be sent to interested parties through a podcast feed, which allows the material to be downloaded to the user's computer.

"Smart" Toys

Each year toys are being produced for young children that have embedded computer chips that activate the toy. There is discussion about the usefulness of these "smart" toys during the early childhood years as compared to the more traditional toys, such as blocks and clay. There isn't much debate, however, about the growing availability of electronically activated interactive toys for very young children. Toddlers now come to early childhood education settings as experienced practitioners of toys they can make "go" and are excited by other forms of technology.

What additional considerations should be made when using digital technology?

Consent

When using any digital image of any person, it is important to get consent for its use. Teachers and caregivers are advised to develop a simple photo release form, which delineates the possible use(s) of the pictures. Parents or guardians should be given a range of options for the possible uses of their children's work and photographic representations. They can then select and indicate their approval of specific purposes by initialing or declining and then signing and dating the form. For example, a parent may choose to give consent for photographs to be used in curriculum projects and the child's portfolio but not in a newsletter or classroom

Web site. All children, staff, volunteers, and parents who appear in photographs should have a photo release on file with the program.

Privacy

Schools and child-care facilities should consider the addition of a policy on protection of privacy to the organization's policy and procedures manual. As part of the statement on how the child and family privacy rights will be protected, information should be provided on how digital images will be used and safeguarded.

Teachers and providers need to take particular care when using any image via the Internet. When school personnel choose to have a Web site or use webcams, they need to be sure they have a secure server and provide protected access.

2

Standards, Assessment, and Documentation

STANDARDS, ASSESSMENT, AND DOCUMENTATION INTRODUCTION

Since the first edition of this book, there has been a seismic shift in educational expectation regarding assessment, evaluation, and documentation. Now teachers from preschool to graduate school are expected to demonstrate that their students are learning. The "standards movement" grew out of public policy debates and growing dissatisfaction with the quality of student progress at all levels of public education. Its goal has been worthy: to improve student outcomes for all children, regardless of their backgrounds and risk factors. The trend toward assessment, the increased need for documentation, and the implementation of standards has caused early childhood educators to think carefully about these topics and what is both useful and appropriate for young children, their families, and their caregivers.

What is assessment?

"Assessment," on the one hand, is a judgment about something based on an understanding of the situation. Other understandings refer to assessment as a method of evaluating student performance or, in an even more specific context, as a calculation of the value of something in order to know how much tax must be paid. All of these definitions denote measurement. Documentation is the record of those measurements, serving as a record of achievement and change over time.

Why is assessment important?

Assessment serves many purposes, but for a teacher the most profound is that of informing instruction. Assessment is embedded in the very act of instruction, as the teacher observes students engaged in the process of learning and evaluates their progress. Obstacles to the acquisition of a new concept or skill are noted, points in need of clarification are gathered, questions on the effectiveness of the presentation and methodology are pondered, and individual progress of the students toward mastery are recorded. These mental notations and physical notes form the foundation of the *assess-assist cycle* that is the hallmark of good instruction. The teacher assesses the status of individual and/or group knowledge, determines what is next to be learned, provides the needed assistance to instruct or clarify the point, and then observes how the students are able to apply the new information. Assessment is important because, when done well, it is the core of good teaching.

What is developmentally appropriate assessment?

Young children are notoriously poor test takers. Evaluation and assessment of young children are challenging under the best of circumstances. It is imperative that early childhood educators think carefully about how to gather and evaluate information for the purposes of assessment. Using play-based or "authentic" assessment, rooted in careful observation and record keeping, yields useful information, particularly when the data are gathered over time (NAEYC[a]). For more details on assessment and particular learning standards for early childhood education, visit the National Association for the Education of Young Children (NAEYC) Web site at http://www.naeyc.org.

Why use systematic observation in assessment?

One of the most powerful tools a teacher or caregiver has at her disposal, second only to the formation of a solid relationship with young children, is high-quality observation over time. Clinical observation requires the teacher to watch and listen to students carefully and critically as they are engaged in learning tasks. Careful observation obliges the observer to focus exclusively on a child or small group and to notice the details of how each student approaches the learning task. The information gleaned from this type of considered observation can inform instruction and provide useful information for assessing each child's progress toward clearly defined learning objectives.

Can technology facilitate appropriate assessment and documentation?

Still and video images record and communicate information in ways that words alone cannot. The visual impact of a moment captured in time is powerful, underscores verbal points, and can serve as a point of discussion. In terms of assessment and documentation, one picture really is worth a thousand words.

A portfolio that captures a representative sample of a child's growth and development is an effective method of documentation. The child's skills are displayed through transcribed language samples, assessment results, observation narratives, and samples of the child's work. Each entry into the portfolio helps the teacher construct a portrait of the child at work in the classroom. Photographs and both audio and video recordings of the child engaged in various learning activities in an educational setting add to the overall picture of the child's school life. While they can be time-consuming to assemble, portfolios offer the opportunity to capture a representative sample of a child's learning style, preferences, and capabilities. They offer the added advantage of being consumer friendly, and present information in a format that tends to be more easily understood by family members.

What are standards?

Various types of standards have evolved over time. When referring to the term "standards" it is useful to be clear on precisely what is being considered. Barbara Bowman, in the September 2006 issue of *Young Children,* describes these considerations in "Standards at the Heart of Educational Equity" as follows:

1. *Learning or Performance Standards,* defining what a student should know or be able to do, represent desired learning outcomes that can be measured and evaluated.

2. *Content Standards* represent specific knowledge, skills, and concepts that students need to master in order to reach the desired educational outcomes. Those standards are usually defined as expectations to be achieved by the end of a specific grade level or time period.

3. *Program Standards* define what program systems and structures need to be in place to create the learning environment needed for children to reach the desired educational outcomes. These may include the organization of time, space and materials, groupings, types of activities, and credential requirements.

4. *Professional Development Standards* are generally tied to accreditation and are often used to chart the course for training institutions. They identify the required skills and knowledge teachers need in order to be effective.

A fifth type of standard to be considered in any discussion of the topic, first introduced by authors Tharp et al. in *Teaching Transformed: Achieving Excellence, Fairness, Inclusion and Harmony* (Westview, 2000), is described as follows:

5. *Standards of Effective Pedagogy* represent a focus on teachers' methods and the strategies they use to implement these strategies. The quality of the classroom experience is deeply impacted by both what the teachers do and how they do it (Tharp et al, 2000).

Pedagogy is the science of instruction. Determining how the teacher organizes and presents that instruction is vitally important in any discussion of standards and the goal of improved student outcomes (Entz, 2007). The research on instruction is clear. How teachers organize instruction and interact with students during that instruction has a profound impact on student outcomes. When teachers employ specific teaching techniques, all students—even those at greatest risk for educational failure—have improved academic outcomes. These techniques cluster around five principles:

1. Teachers and students work together to produce a common product. (Joint Productive Activity)

2. Teachers recognize that language is a metagoal, embedding and emphasizing both language learning and literacy in all activities throughout the day. (Language and Literacy Across the Curriculum)

3. Teachers help students to see the application and relevance of their learning by connecting academic lessons to students' lives. (Contextualization/Making Meaning)

4. Teachers create lessons that are intellectually challenging. (Cognitive Challenge)

5. Teachers recognize that conversation is a powerful tool and teach through dialogue. (Instructional Conversation).

These five standards of effective pedagogy are embedded in each of the lessons in this book.

How do standards impact assessment?

Standards offer a structure for organizing the assessment information to be gathered, the skills to be taught, the observations to be made, and the portfolios to be developed. If, for example, a teacher wanted to create a professional portfolio for the purpose of obtaining a Child Development Associate (CDA) credential, then organizing the portfolio entries into the thirteen functional areas that define the CDA process would make sense. The emphasis of a child's portfolio to be shared with parents, reflecting progress toward the mastery of performance standards, would be organized around the desired learning outcomes. While not limited to the structure of a particular standard, it does offer a starting point in the planning, instructional activities, assessment, and documentation.

How are the checklists and content standards used?

One method of using the checklists in this book is to create crosswalks that connect the skills listed in each chapter with the state or local content standards or the content standards developed by specific professional organizations (NAEYC[b]). (A comprehensive list of links to national standards, along with extensive resources for early childhood teachers, can be found at http://www.naeyc.org/ece/ on the Web site for the National Association for the Education of Young Children.) A format for the crosswalk, listing the checklist items in a left hand column and items from a set of content standards in a corresponding column on the right, is illustrated in Chart 2.1.

Chart 2.1   Sample Crosswalk Between Checklists and Standards

A Crosswalk Linking Checklist in Picture This and a Representative Sample of Standards	
Checklist Items From *Picture This* Emerging Literacy: Writing	NAEYC: Continuum of Children's Development in Early Reading and Writing
Sample: Writing Activities encourage children to • Watch adult writers • Ask what an adult is writing	Phase 1: Awareness and Exploration Goals For Preschool: Children can • Enjoy listening to and discussing storybooks • Understand that print carries a message

(Continued)

Chart 2.1 (Continued)

A Crosswalk Linking Checklist in Picture This and a Representative Sample of Standards	
Checklist Items From *Picture This* Emerging Literacy: Writing	NAEYC: Continuum of Children's Development in Early Reading and Writing
• Ask to be read what has been written • Dictate words to be written by others • Write, although not legible by others • Copy letters • Form identifiable letters from memory • Copy one's own name • Write one's own name • Write individual words • Express thoughts and feelings in writing • Collect one's own writing in book form	• Engage in reading and writing attempts • Identify labels and signs in the environment • Participate in rhyming games • Identify some letters and make some letter sounds • Use known letters and make some letter-sound matches • Use known letters or approximations of letters to represent written language (especially meaningful words like their names and phrases such as "I love you")
	Hawaii Preschool Content Standard Writing Standard Standard #6: Show an interest in writing.

It is clear that some form of assessment, documentation, and adherence to standards will be a part of most formal educational programs, including early childhood programs, for the foreseeable future. Used wisely, educators can use these changes in practice to enhance their relationships with their students, to inform their teaching, to help children learn more efficiently, and to communicate more effectively with families.

PROFESSIONAL PORTFOLIO

Skill

Assessment: articulation and presentation of professional competence

Objectives

1. To document professional competencies across a range of teaching skills

2. To present indicators of competence in a visually attractive format

Description

Increasingly, teachers are being urged to compile a portfolio that represents an overview of their teaching. These professional portfolios can be used to secure new teaching appointments and to pursue advancement within an organization. Some institutions require the preparation and periodic revision of a professional portfolio as a condition of employment. Fortunately, teachers can use many of the digital photographs taken during classroom activities and the preparation of student portfolios to demonstrate their professional competence.

The first step is to identify the areas that need to be featured in the portfolio. Some schools provide an outline of areas to be covered, while other organizations use the rubrics described by professional organizations. Students in training and teachers should consult their own institutions to determine the material to be covered in a professional portfolio. Examples of topics to be included in different types of portfolios can be found in the materials presented by the following organizations, which can be found on their respective Web sites.

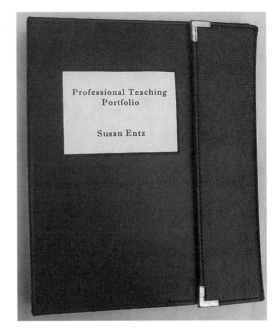

1. The Child Development Associate (CDA) Credentialing Program has identified thirteen functional areas of competence to be covered in the written presentation for credentialing. (http://www.cdacouncil.org/)

2. The National Association For The Education of Young Children has articulated standards with The Interstate New Teacher Assessment and Support Consortium (INTASC) to identify key elements to be included in a professional teaching portfolio. (http://www.ccsso.org)

3. The National Board for Professional Teaching Standards provides key elements to be included in the preparation of a portfolio. (http://www.nbpts.org/)

Once the format has been determined, the teacher writes a description of her professional competence in that area. She may also find an existing picture or take new photographs to support the some of the entries in the portfolio. Samples of her work should also be included, and that work can sometimes be depicted best in a photograph. When completed, the educator has a collection of her work that represents in words and pictures the best of her teaching.

STUDENT PORTFOLIOS

Skill

Documentation: measurement of student progress against an articulated standard

Objectives

1. To document the child's current developmental status in a variety of domains

2. To assess the child's progress against a standard

3. To present evidence of the child's progress in an authentic manner

4. To identify and record the child's skills as well as any deficiencies

5. To present indicators of achievement in a visually attractive format

6. To create a vehicle for the discussion a child's performance with parents that is organized and illustrative of the child's skills

Description

Authentic assessment refers to an approach to assessment and documentation that is meaningful. The teacher applies assessment criteria in ways that may elicit and reflect the student's true abilities. Using this approach, the children are engaged in complex or contextualized tasks that enable them to demonstrate their competence in the natural or authentic setting.

Once the teacher has identified the domains, specific learning objectives, and skills to be documented, she can set up a planning matrix. By listing the targeted skills down the left side and the names of the children in the group across the top, the teacher can check off the tasks per child that have been observed and documented.

During the day, the teacher observes actions or events to be recalled and snaps a picture of that scene. She may use note cards or sticky notes to jot down brief reminders of each event and any direct quotes that she may want to recall. When time allows, the teacher can then download the photographs and record the identifying data (name, date, location, activity) and the targeted skill. The transcribed notes and direct quotes from the event provide details and context for that skill. The teacher can then determine whether this illustration represents a newly emerging skill, a task on which the child is progressing, or one that has been mastered.

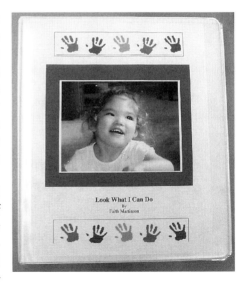

A variety of entries are recorded over a period of time and added to the portfolio. Samples of work, scanned pictures of drawings and other arwork, video and audio recording, and other representations of the child's abilities are recorded and saved as well. Checklists, narratives, and other forms of evaluation can be included.

Children may also be invited to aid in the development of their portfolios. They can use a classroom camera to take pictures of objects or activities that are of interest to them. Students can also document work with which they are particularly pleased. Once the pictures are downloaded and printed, the children are invited to dictate descriptions for their photographs as yet another example of their expressive language skills.

When viewed as a whole, the portfolio should give a visual impression of the child's abilities and challenges. Each entry should tell a little story about a meaningful event at school. The portfolio is shared with each child's parents at conferences throughout the year and sent home at the end of the year as a permanent remembrance of the child's school experiences.

FUNFOLIOS

Skill

Documentation: single-subject performance

Objectives

1. To document a child's progress in a particular area of the curriculum

2. To introduce the teacher or caregiver to the process of using photographic logs to document developmental progress

Description

When a multisubject child portfolio seems too daunting an undertaking, teachers and caregivers may choose to make a more abbreviated version. This technique for making and recording systematic observations is similar to the more expansive documentation of a full child portfolio, but the size and scope of a "Funfolio" is more modest.

The teacher might begin the process of authentic assessment by focusing on only one area of the curriculum. She would write up a description of that subject area, describing for the parent in general terms what might be learned and why that area of development is important. Over the course of several days, the teacher observes the children as they engage in activities that utilize these skills. Entries for the Funfolio consist of photographs depicting the child's abilities in this area of development, brief accompanying descriptions, and samples of their work where appropriate. A simple checklist or rating scale of age-appropriate skills in this domain can also be included.

Children's artwork makes an attractive cover for these simple Funfolios. Have the children draw, paint, or make prints on a sheet of 12 x 18-inch construction paper that will be folded in half to serve as the cover. When the paint or ink is dry, the teacher writes a title and the child's name on the cover. The teacher then stacks the description of the domain and all of the entries in order, inserts them into the folded sheet of construction paper, and staples along the folded edge to make a booklet.

SITE-VISIT REPORT

Skill

Documentation: informal observation

Objectives

1. To observe current levels of learning
2. To document current levels of learning
3. To identify strategies of instruction
4. To provide families and caregivers with concrete information on instruction
5. To identify staff training needs

Description

Many early childhood programs occur in sites other than a school setting. Outside consultants and support staff are sometimes available to make site visits to assist the early childhood educator with individual children or to make program suggestions.

Informal assessment and documentation are important in these settings because they provide accurate information to share with parents about how to facilitate their child's overall development. Through the site report, the consultant can assist the early childhood educators in developing their abilities to do systematic observations. Some home-care providers and teachers of young children find that the process of consultation and systematic observation identifies for them areas in which they would like to pursue additional training.

Child:	Kamakoa	Date of Observation:	3/6/08
Date of Birth:	5/17/05	Chronological Age:	33 mos.
Observed By:	Developmental Specialist	Location:	Day Care

The purpose of this visit was to observe Kamakoa's fine motor skills during daily routines. He was playing near two other children on the floor when the observer arrived.

Snap Beads

Kamakoa smiled a greeting but then went back to the large pop-beads that he was playing with. He had sufficient hand and finger strength to grasp the beads and to pull them apart. He needs more practice to recognize that the knob end of one bead goes into the hole of the other in order to make them snap back together.

Puzzles

Kamakoa was eager to attempt the large noninterlocking wooden puzzle. He immediately picked up the puzzle board and placed it on his lap. He used his preferred hand, his right, to grasp the small knobs on the individual puzzle pieces. As seen in this picture, Kamakoa is not yet using a neat pincer grasp to pick up small objects. Instead, he tends to "rake" at the object to be picked up and then use all of his fingers to surround it. He was successful in removing the puzzle pieces using this approach. He was not yet able to match the animal pieces to their forms on the puzzle board.

Through careful observation, the consultant and provider can develop information on the child's "instructional range." By noting what skills the child can do easily on his own, toys and activities can be provided in the child's "independent range" of learning. This information is useful for parents and caregivers for those times when they need to be occupied with other children or other tasks. Noting the instructional range of learning helps providers and parents to recognize the activities that engage the child but are too difficult for him to do completely on his own; these represent opportunities for adults to teach new skills. It is also useful to note which activities require skills that are still too difficult for the child and will cause frustration; these represent the "frustration level" of instruction.

Short descriptions of the child's skills during the playgroup or home visit can be recorded and augmented by an illustrative photograph. Suggestions for how to capitalize on the particular stage of development noted can then be included. These reports by consultants or support staff can serve as a model for the provider's own observations.

Individual entries of the site visits and ongoing observations can be put into plastic page protectors and inserted into a sectioned three-ring binder. Over time, this collection will create a montage of the child's interests, abilities, and challenges.

By analyzing the portfolio entries and assessment findings, early childhood educators often identify topics for staff training or parent education workshops. For example, when reviewing a site-visit report of a child attempting a craft project at a library story time, it was noted that the child was having difficulty with a cut-and-paste project. An activity was created to help the parent assist this child to learn how to use a glue stick.

STAGES OF SOCIAL PLAY

Skill

Assessment: social play skills

Objectives

1. To identify the predominant stage of social play

2. To identify emerging stages of social play

3. To document growth over time in social play

Description

Play has been described as the work of childhood. It is important for those working with young children to understand the importance of play in the early childhood curriculum, how to utilize play to achieve instructional objectives, and how to assist children in mastering each stage of play.

In a historical context, in 1932, M. B. Parten defined stages of play in terms of the interaction and social relationships among the participants. The various types of social play can be placed along a continuum from the least amount of engagement to playful interactions that require the most amount of social sophistication. Parten's stages include the following:

1. Unoccupied Behavior—children are disengaged (i.e., wander aimlessly or stare blankly into space).

2. Onlooker Behavior—children observe but do not attempt to join in or interact with others.

3. Solitary Play—children play independently and apart from others, concentrating on their own objects and movements.

4. Parallel Play—children play independently in the company of others but with them only occasionally or not at all.

5. Associative Play—children play near and sometimes interact with others and may use the same or similar toys or materials in play, but with no sustained plan or cooperation.

6. Cooperative Play—children plan, assign roles, coordinate their actions, and contribute to carrying out the plan or achieving a common goal.

Observe children at play and take candid photographs that represent each child's typical stage of social play. Format a report page in a page layout program with space for the child's name, age and date of observation. Provide a continuum of social play, with space for a check mark. Then import a representative photograph and write a brief description of the child's observed play behavior. Include this page in the child's portfolio and reassess quarterly to document progress.

STAGES OF COGNITIVE PLAY

Skill

Assessment: cognitive play stages

Objectives

1. To identify the predominant stage of cognitive play

2. To identify emerging stages of cognitive play

3. To document growth in cognitive play over time

Description

Another way to look at children's play is to analyze how play reflects a child's cognitive abilities. Building on the work of Jean Piaget and, later, Sara Smilansky, we can identify a conceptual framework that traces the child's cognitive skills through a range of increasingly more complex levels of play (in Feeney, 2006, p. 171).

1. Exploratory (sensorimotor) Play—children explore objects through movement and their senses.

2. Functional Play—children examine objects to determine their function, manipulate them to find their functional side, and explore what they can make the objects do.

3. Symbolic Play—children engage in pretend play, assuming roles and using toys or other objects to represent objects they would use in real life.

4. Constructive Play—children use real objects to build an object or create a construction according to a plan.

5. Games With Rules—children recognize and eventually follow preset rules of a game.

Children frequently move in and out of various stages of cognitive play during a single play period. For example, when a wand magnet is introduced into play, a child might first explore the wand by looking at it, feeling the heavier end, and then waving it back and forth in the air. Once the sensory aspects of the magnet have been identified, the child's attention will be turned to its functional aspects. How the magnet is attracted to metal objects is learned through experimentation, as the child builds up a mental representation of the magnetic properties of the object. Later that same day, the child might incorporate his knowledge of the magnet into his imaginative play.

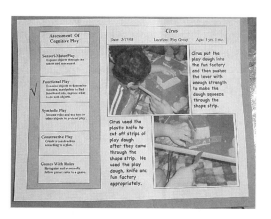

Create an observational guide that lists the elements of cognitive play, with sufficient space for writing notes on how the child approaches play. Select a representative photograph to import into the formatted guide and record observations about the stage(s) of cognitive play that were seen in that vignette.

CHECKLIST-PLUS

Skill

Assessment: specific skills

Objectives

1. To provide supplementary information to support the checklist assessment

2. To save images of children's work products for late analysis and comparison

Description

Use the checklists provided in each chapter in this book or other developmental checklists to provide a quick overview of a child's performance in a particular area of the curriculum or developmental domain.

Supplement the information gleaned from the checklist with candid photographs of the child demonstrating proficiency with particular skills. A photograph of the child holding the scissors and cutting in a straight line, for example, is an effective way to demonstrate improved motor planning and eye-hand coordination. The same child completing a shape formboard provides valuable information on solving visual problems, awareness of spatial relations, and matching shapes.

A scanned image of the child's work product is another effective way to document what the child has done. The scanned image is particularly useful when the teacher wants a sample of the child's work but the child wants to take it home to share with the family. By scanning the drawing, writing, or project, the teacher retains a permanent record for later use while accommodating the child's wishes.

Visual images, whether photographic, scanned, or in other formats, support the written assessment and communicate more information to parents or colleagues than would the printed word alone.

Mathematics Checklist

Child: Danny_____

	Baseline __/__/__	Period 1 __/__/__	Period 2 __/__/__

Spatial Relations and Geometry

Skill	Baseline	Period 1	Period 2
To associate a part to its whole	−		
To solve visual problems	− +		
To become aware of spatial relations	−		
To match shapes	− +		
To form shapes	−		
To count the sides of shapes	− +		
To match three-dimensional shapes with their two-dimensional pictures	−		

Danny used the trial-and-error method to solve this visual problem. He did not survey the forms to find the shape in his hand before he tried to fit it into a space. He was eventually able to place these three basic shapes.

BEHAVIORAL SNAPSHOTS

Skill

Assessment: behavioral development

Objectives

1. To observe and document challenging behaviors
2. To make behaviors clear and understandable to teaching staff, family, and others working with the child
3. To analyze and further understanding of the purpose(s) of the behaviors
4. To suggest alternative strategies

Description

Often, problems in the classroom are behavioral rather than academic. Learning occurs in a social environment, and even very young children need to develop adequate social skills. They also need to develop strategies for negotiating with other children and managing their own emotions and behavioral responses.

Observation of typical classroom behaviors frequently provides an informational treasure trove that can shed light on how to proceed with the children in question. Understanding the context of a particular behavior, what the children were doing, and how they were acting before an incident of inappropriate behavior provide useful clues. A record of behavioral challenges over time helps the teacher to notice patterns and serves as the basis for creating an effective intervention strategy.

When a child has sufficient verbal skills to communicate his needs, wants, and feelings, he has the ability to look at pictures of a classroom event after the emotion of the altercation has passed and to talk about what went on. The teacher can label the

Ethan 10/20/07
Behavioral Snapshot

What Occurred?
Ethan was asked to help put away the toys before snack time.

How Did the Child Respond?
Ethan got upset and crawled up on the table and covered his eyes.

Why Do You Think the Behavior Occurred?
Ethan did not want to stop playing.

What Did the Teacher Do?
I let Ethan know that I understood that he was unhappy because he was not finished stringing the beads. It was time to clean up, though. I told him that when he was ready he could pick up his bead basket and join us. Then I ignored him, but watched him out of the corner of my eye.

How Did the Child Respond?
Ethan fussed for about a minute and then climbed off the small table and joined the group. I asked him to get the basket of beads for me and he went to get them. When he brought the beads, he washed his hands and had snack.

emotions if a child does not have the label for that feeling. They can talk about what the child wanted and what else he could have done to meet his needs in a more socially acceptable way. The teacher can help the child role-play alternative actions and practice the words needed to employ the new technique. Over time, this strategy will help children to build a repertoire of skills they can use in similar situations should they occur in the future.

That technique is greatly enhanced by the addition of a few photographs. The pictures can be used to talk about the incident with the child and shared with staff to develop strategies for handling future incidents consistently and appropriately. It is also an effective and more visual way to share information with parents.

Behavioral snapshots are an example of an effective *assess-assist cycle*, because the information gleaned from the informal assessment is used immediately to assist the child in altering his behavior. The child can be further assessed to determine whether he was able to internalize the changes suggested by the teacher's intervention or whether further instruction would be needed.

KINDERGARTEN READINESS

Skill

Documentation: observation of competence for kindergarten

Objectives

1. To identify, for parents of children entering kindergarten, the skills and abilities that will be expected in school so they may be practiced at home

2. To underscore, for preschool teachers and care providers, the skills and abilities thought to be important in successful transitions into kindergarten

3. To share information and activities with parents that promote the development of critical skills and abilities

Description

Almost all states have adopted content standards for four-year-olds, and most departments of education have identified criteria to identify the readiness of incoming kindergarteners. Many school districts have "Kindergarten Fairs" or "Readiness Days" in which parents and children of incoming kindergarteners can visit the classroom and engage in sample activities.

Posters labeling each area with corresponding skills can be matched with photographs of children engaged appropriately in those activities. This format can be used to organize the flow of parents and children through a variety of activity center and interest areas. The critical skill(s) to be developed are identified.

A take-home handout with photographs illustrating each critical area of development helps parents remember to practice some of the important skills before their child heads off to the first day of kindergarten.

POWERPOINT SLIDE SHOW

Skill

Documentation: creation of a multimedia system

Objectives

1. To link standards, assessment, and documentation

2. To present a sample of the child's developmental skills in a visually pleasing format

3. To describe and highlight in simple, understandable terms key facets of development

Description

A presentation program, such as PowerPoint, can be used to format the key developmental points to be featured in the slide show. A presentation emphasizing standards for the development of mathematical thinking, for example, might highlight the five key areas of mathematics that have been identified as important for young children by the National Council for the Teachers of Mathematics: Number and Operation, Geometry and Spatial, Measurement, Patterns and Algebra, and Analyzing and Displaying Data. The reading presentation might underscore the key developmental points from the Early Literacy Standard. Clip art or scanned images can be added to the chapter title pages.

After the program has been prepared, the teacher can set up mathematical activities

that will prompt the child to exhibit behaviors that represent mathematical thinking. They might, for example, be asked to match or sort objects or create interesting patterns with blocks. Activities of daily living that feature the key areas of mathematics can also be recorded. Photographs, scanned images, and video clips can be imported into the formatted program to highlight the child's progress in this area of development.

The presentation can be shown at a parent conference to highlight particular areas of the child's development. Teachers can burn a copy of the slide show onto a CD for the parents to take home.

E-FOLIOS

Skill

Documentation: creation of video portfolios

Objectives

1. To capture representative episodes, illustrating the child's typical classroom performances

2. To organize the video footage for ease of use, storage, and sharing

3. To share specific facets of a child's development, behavior, and academic performance with the family

Description

Video is a dramatic and powerful medium for recording children's approaches to learning, behaviors during an activity, and progress toward a desired and measurable outcome. An incident captured in real time can demonstrate key points that no verbal description can match.

A major disadvantage of working with video shot in the classroom, however, is the time it takes to edit the footage and find the short snippets needed to include in a video presentation of the child's developmental, behavioral, or academic status. To offset this drawback, the teacher needs to plan well in advance. By knowing what aspects of the child's performance to look for when shooting the footage, the teacher can reduce the editing time to a manageable level.

The key footage is imported into a moviemaking application. The teacher can do a simple voice-over, describing what is happening or what will be seen in the next scene. A

music track, title slides, and other techniques can be added to increase the effectiveness of the movie being created.

Copies of the e-portfolio can be shared with the family and used for staff training.

ACCREDITATION PORTFOLIO

Skill

Documentation: creation of portfolio for program standards

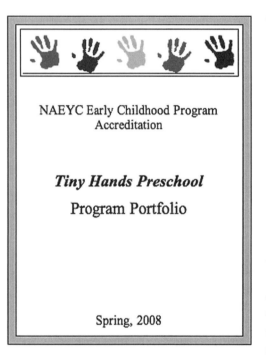

Objectives

1. To detail how a school or program meets established criteria and program standards

2. To provide supplementary information for accreditation review

3. To use photographs to highlight various aspects of the program

Description

Program accreditation and reaccreditation are complex and time-consuming processes. The required material is specifically delineated, but can be supplemented with photographic images of specific elements of the program that staff would like to emphasize. Pictures can be included in the program binder highlighting areas of particular importance to the school or staff.

Program photographs taken for accreditation can also be used for parents' night, newsletters, and open houses to share the pride of accomplishment for different aspects of the program.

3

Language

LANGUAGE INTRODUCTION

What is language?

"Language" is a system of symbols agreed on by a group of people to represent objects, concepts, and experiences. Language is represented by words, and a precise set of rules governs their combination. Language is composed of two parts: "receptive language" (listening) and "expressive language" (speaking).

Why is language learning important?

Learning to use language is the preeminent human accomplishment. It is important for three reasons.

1. The purpose of language is communication and social interaction with other people. It allows us to express our needs, wants, and concerns; to direct others; to direct our own behavior; to describe or explain events; to question; and to relate to others.

2. Very early in human development, young children learn to think in words. This fusion of thought and language emerges as inner speech that lasts a lifetime.

3. Language is important diagnostically because children's verbalizations provide insight into what the children know and understand about the world. The development of language makes it possible to trace a child's movement from the concrete to the abstract and from a description of the here and now to the contemplation of past and future occurrences or of fantasy.

Individuals with weak language skills face social, emotional, academic, and intellectual challenges throughout life. Poor listening and verbal skills take a toll on children's social relationships. Children with these poor skills often have difficulty joining others at play, maintaining their end of a conversation, staying on track, asking relevant questions, negotiating, or solving problems. Because the consequences of a language delay or disorder are so significant, it is important that help for children be sought when signs are noticed.

How is language learned?

Language acquisition is an intricate dance between genetic predisposition and social engagement. Children are born with the capacity to learn language. But although humans are "hardwired" to listen and to speak, children must have the opportunity to use their equipment. They need to be actively engaged in language-based interactions with caring adults. By using gestures, facial expressions, sounds, intonations, words, and sentences, young children construct their own understanding of language.

Language is intrinsically motivating. Babies gurgle and coo because they enjoy the physical sensation of speech. They quickly learn that these sounds bring a positive reaction from that soft, sweet-smelling person who provides food and cares for them. Speaking is a skill that requires a great deal of practice. Fortunately, it is so rewarding that most children are motivated to expend the energy to do so.

Language follows a predictable sequence. The timetable may vary slightly from child to child, but the sequence remains constant. Cooing precedes babbling and single-word utterances, which predate two-word phrases, simple sentences, and complex sentences. Each affects the development of the stage that follows.

How is language development facilitated?

A caring adult—whether teacher, caregiver, or parent—needs to provide a safe, secure, and loving environment in which talking and listening can occur. Children who are fearful or preoccupied are not available for language learning.

Provide a language-rich environment with a variety of interesting things for children to see, touch, smell, hear, taste, do, and talk about. Language is learned best when people talk about real objects or events that are truly of interest to them. Provide as many firsthand experiences as possible and explore these topics in enough depth to help children develop a meaningful vocabulary for describing their experiences.

Schedule time for meaningful conversation and contemplation. Facilitate discussion between both adults and children and among the children themselves. Encourage children to make choices and decisions, with frequent opportunities to discuss with, explain to, or teach another.

In conversation, model appropriate language usage. Use vocabulary slightly beyond the child's current level, adjust sentence structure to the child's current capacity to comprehend, ask open-ended questions, share feelings, use rich language to direct or describe, and offer opinions. Answering a child's questions acknowledges both the initiative and the effort required to ask them. Formulate answers on the level of the child's understanding.

Remember that young children learn best when they explore ideas in a holistic way. A thematic unit or the project approach allows children to integrate listening, speaking, reading, writing, mathematics, science, and the other curriculum areas in a natural, meaningful way.

Most of all, make language learning enjoyable.

LIGHTS, CAMERA, ACTION

Skill

Language: action words (verbs)

Objectives

1. To experience the meaning of verbs physically

2. To follow directions using action words

3. To identify named verbs in pictures

4. To describe actions in pictures

Description

Invite children to participate in a particular movement. For example, say, *Let's all jump up and down together. Jump, jump, jump.* Take candid photographs of individual children as they perform this motion.

Print, mount on cards, and laminate the photos. Then, share them with the group. Have each child select a card at random and describe what is pictured on that card. For example, *In this picture, Jennifer is jumping.*

Use the pictures to lead morning exercises or to get the wigglies out at circle time. Have the leader choose a card, identify the motion, and lead the group in that action.

Repeat this process with other actions: clapping, climbing, rolling, pouring, stirring, hopping, twisting, bending, and winking.

Extensions

Small-Group Activities

Select six photographs of actions and insert them into a page layout program so that there are three photos across in two rows. Print two copies. Mount one copy on construction paper to make a game board; laminate it. Cut the other copy into its six individual pictures; mount the pictures on construction paper to make picture playing cards and then laminate them. Repeat with several other sets of photographs to make four to six sets of game boards and picture cards. To play a lotto game, place the cards facedown on the table. With a game board for each player, have one child select a picture card and name the action word depicted by the photograph. Tell each child with that word on his or her game board to cover it with a button or paper token. The player whose game board is filled first is the "first winner." Continue to play until all children are "winners."

Independent Explorations

Place the photographs into a basket for the children to sort. For example, a child can sort them by actions: all pictures of children running in one pile, all those of children clapping in another, and so on.

One-on-One Instruction

Receptive Language: Place several action pictures in front of the child and name one. Ask the child to find it. For example, say, *Find the picture of pouring.*

Expressive Language: Show the child a picture and ask the child to answer a question. For example, ask, *What is _____ [Patty] doing?*

Family Involvement

Print a set of photographs for each child and send them home in an envelope. Include instructions to an adult to encourage the child to describe what is pictured.

WHERE'S THE BEAR?

Skill

Language: position words (prepositions)

Objectives

1. To place a teddy bear in a named position

2. To name the position the teddy bear is in

3. To point to the picture that depicts the bear in a named position

4. To name the position of the bear in a photograph

5. To match pictures of bears by the positions they are in

Description

Use a young child's attachment to teddy bears to explore position words. Ask each child to bring a favorite teddy bear, other stuffed animal, or doll from home; introduce it to the group. For example, say, *This is Fuzzy Brown Bear. He was very excited to come to school today.*

Tell the children that the bears want to show the class how to play a new game. With your own bear, lead the children through a variety of movements that include prepositions. For example, say, *Put the bear "over" your head, "between" your legs, "behind" your back, "under" your arm, then "on" your shoulder.*

During center time, set up a photo studio where individual children can pose their bears. Take photographs of several children placing their bears in particular locations (e.g., *Put your bear "next to" the fish tank. Hide your bear "under" the chair. Take your bear "through" the playhouse door. Put your bear "on" the tricycle.*). Print, mount on cards, and laminate the pictures.

Each day during this project, ask a few children to show the pictures of their bears and to describe where their bears are.

Extensions

Small-Group Activities

Encourage children to take their bears to the housekeeping and other dramatic play areas to stimulate their use of position words and include them during play.

Independent Explorations

Place sets of cards out for children to sort by (a) bear ownership, (b) pictured locations, or (c) types of bears.

One-on-One Instruction

Receptive Language: Place all of one child's bear photographs on the table and name one of the positions. Say, *Show me the picture of you putting Fuzzy Brown Bear "on" the tricycle.* Ask the child to point to that picture.

Expressive Language: Encourage the child to talk to the bear as a parent would to a small child, describing its pictures to the bear. For example, *Look, Fuzzy, here is a picture of you "on" the tricycle.*

Family Involvement

Send the child's bear and photographs home and invite parents to look at the pictures with their child and to talk about the positions of the bear. Suggest that they direct their child to place the bear in the home environment by using the same positions. For example, they can say, *Put Fuzzy Brown Bear "on" the sofa.*

PHOTO SHOOT

Skill

Language: labeling objects

Objectives

1. To match three-dimensional objects

2. To name three-dimensional objects

3. To match photographs with their three-dimensional objects

4. To match photographs of objects

5. To name objects in photographs

Description

Help toddlers and young preschoolers see the relationship between real objects and two-dimensional representations by inviting the children to help with a photo shoot. Put out an array of objects that represent the target words to be learned. Have each child pick an object he would like photographed. Allow the child to help photograph it.

Take the children to the computer so that they can assist in the printing. Talk about the items during the printing process (e.g., *Let's do Kalei's picture next. Kalei, what was your object? Oh, that's right. Kalei took a picture of a snake.*). Print two copies of each picture and mount them as cards.

Put out the objects that were photographed and have each child in turn select a facedown card. Ask the child to identify the pictured object and to put it by its three-dimensional object.

Extensions

Small-Group Activities

Work with the group to create a second set of object photographs.

Independent Explorations

Place a set of objects and pictures in the activity center for matching.

One-on-One Instruction

Receptive Language: Put out the set of objects used in the photo shoot. Ask the child to point to each object as you name it. Next, hand the child a picture card to be placed by its object. Finally, work only with the set of pictures; have the child hand you a picture that you name.

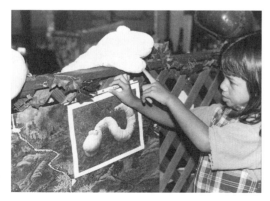

Expressive Language: Show the child the key objects, then pick up or point to one, and ask the child to talk about it. If she is unable to name the object, give a clue. Point to the picture of the apple, saying, *It's an "ap...."* If the child is still unable to retrieve the word, provide it, use it in a sentence, and then name it again (e.g., *Apple. This is an apple. Apple.*). Encourage the child to repeat the word.

Family Involvement

Invite parents to send to school common objects they would like their child to know how to name. Work with the child to make the set of photographs and send home the object picture sets, with directions for the parents on how to use them effectively.

PICTURE THIS

Skill

Language: verbal expression

Objectives

1. To develop verbal expressive skills

2. To develop aesthetic appreciation

3. To develop self-confidence

Description

Work with pairs of children to identify objects, people, events, or places they find interesting and would like to photograph. Talk with them about how to set up each picture, whether it should be a close-up or a wide-angle shot. Allow the children to take the shots, with assistance if necessary.

Take the children to the computer, download the photographs into a page layout program, and work with the children to place each picture and then create effects and text for the rest of the page.

During group time, ask each child to share his or her page and to describe it, tell why it is of interest, and explain the process used to create it.

Extensions

Small-Group Activities

Have the children in the group interview the designer of each page, formulating questions and listening carefully to the answers.

Independent Explorations

Put the pictures displayed during group time in the learning center for individual investigation and discussion.

One-on-One Instruction

Receptive Language: Play a game of "I Spy With My Own Little Eye" with the child's own work. Select a photograph to be described in rich detail so that the child is able to identify it from the clues.

Expressive Language: Have each child evaluate his or her work, deciding which is liked best and why. Ask each child to select the best samples to be included in his or her yearlong portfolio collection.

Family Involvement

Assemble the photographs designed by each child into individual collections to be sent home as a source of discussion and pride.

LEARNING LOTTO

Skill

Language: vocabulary development

Objectives

1. To name pictured items relating to a current theme or unit

2. To describe the physical attributes of the pictured item

3. To describe the function of a pictured item

Description

When considering a new theme or unit of study, brainstorm and list all new vocabulary words the children will need. Identify those objects or processes that can be photographed and take those pictures as the unit progresses.

In a separate page layout program, size the photographs to approximately 1-inch squares. Insert them into a lotto board format of two rows down and three columns across. Print two copies. Laminate both copies and then cut one set into individual playing cards.

Share the game with the whole group, having the children identify the objects or actions and then showing them how to play the game.

Extensions

Small-Group Activities

Work with a small group to identify objects to use for other theme-related lotto games. Encourage children to name the objects and actions as they discuss plans for creating the game.

Independent Explorations

Place the game materials into an envelope in a learning center for individual exploration.

One-on-One Instruction

Receptive Language: Play the game with one child. Place all the individual cards face up on the table. Say, *Find the _____ and put it on the game board.* If the child has difficulty, point to two cards and ask, *Is the _____ this one or that one?*

Expressive Language: Play the game with one child. Before each player can place a game piece on the playing board, he must be able to name it.

Family Involvement

Send home copies of the game with directions written on the outside of the manila envelope containing all the game pieces.

YESTERDAY, TODAY, AND TOMORROW

Skill

Language: verb tense

Objectives

1. To develop an appreciation for the passage of time

2. To sequence events

3. To use regular and irregular past tense verbs correctly

4. To use present and future tenses correctly

Description

Time is an elusive concept for young children, and the language used to describe when events occur is also challenging. Help children develop an understanding of the sequence of events and the words used to describe them.

Make a large pocket chart with three columns. Write "yesterday," "today," and "tomorrow" atop the columns as labels. Glue two or three thin poster board strips below each label. Take photographs of classroom events, print them, and make sentence strip cards to describe the action and the proper tense. For example, write "Yesterday: We finger-painted. Today: We easel-paint. Tomorrow: We will sponge-paint."

During group time, show the photographs from the previous day's events and talk about them, modeling the correct verb usage. Place them in the chart. Next, put up the sentence strips describing the activities. Then, show the photo of today's activity, put it into the chart, and add the sentence strip. Describe today's activities using the present tense. Repeat with tomorrow's activities, using the future tense.

Extensions

Small-Group Activities

Form an activity-planning group, and meet with the group to decide on a few future activities. For example, the group might decide on the snack to serve or the instruments to use to accompany a song. Depending on the maturity of the children in the group, they may even take the photographs.

Independent Explorations

The child may take the photographs out of the chart, mix them up, and then put them back into the correct spot. Make this a self-correcting game by reducing the key photograph, printing it, and gluing it onto the back of the descriptive sentence strip.

One-on-One Instruction

Receptive Language: Spend a few moments with the child looking at the chart. Describe one of the pictures, modeling the correct language. Ask the child to point to the named photograph. For example, say, *Yesterday, Auntie Lani played the ukulele.*

Expressive Language: Point to a picture on the chart and ask a question that places it in time. Have the child answer, using the correct tense. For example, ask, *What special snack will Josh's mom bring tomorrow?*

Family Involvement

Locate the chart near the check-in table and comment on it as the children arrive and depart. Encourage parents to talk about events that have occurred at school that day and that will happen at school tomorrow.

COLOR A RAINBOW

Skill

Language: color words

Objectives

1. To identify objects of a particular color

2. To name objects of a particular color

3. To name photographs of a particular color

4. To group photographs by color

Description

Take the class on a color treasure hunt, having children locate a particular color in objects in their environment. One day, the group might look for red objects and another day focus on things that are purple.

Each day, print the photographs on a color printer. Have the group cut out the pictures.

Make a large outline of a rainbow on butcher paper. Write one color word on the left edge of each color of the arc. Then have the children glue photographs of that color into the correct arc. For example, the yellow arc might be represented with a yellow crayon, marking pen, Lego block, yield sign, and cup from the dramatic play area.

Hang the color rainbow in the room and talk with the children about what they have found that represents the targeted color. Repeat each day, focusing on a different color, then locate objects, take the photographs, and add them to the display.

Extensions

Small-Group Activities

Take a walk with a small group and the camera to find additional objects of a particular color. Add these to the large rainbow chart or have the children make their own color card games from the pictures. To make a Go Fish for Colors game, print four copies of each color photograph, mount each picture on card stock, and play.

Independent Explorations

Prepare a piece of white poster board that has a color word printed on the top and a sample color drawn near it. Provide discarded magazines and catalogs. The child's job is to look through the printed material to find pictures of the designated color and then cut or tear them out and glue them onto the poster.

One-on-One Instruction

Receptive Language: Look at the rainbow display with the child and name pictured objects of different colors. Have the child find the named picture. For example, say, *Where is the yellow chair?*

Expressive Language: Point to a photograph on the rainbow chart and ask the child to name its color. For example, ask, *What color is this chair?*

Family Involvement

Send home a partially completed color poster, as described in the "Receptive Language" section. Ask the parents to work with their child to look through printed material at home to find additional pictures to complete the poster. Encourage the parents to include color words in their daily conversations with their child during this period.

WHOSE SHOES?

Skill

Language: possessive words

Objectives

1. To identify the ownership of objects

2. To use possessive words correctly

Description

Use the camera to take full-body pictures of children and teachers in the class. Visitors dressed in their work uniforms also make good subjects for this activity.

Print each photograph taken. Then, size the picture so that only the shoes are visible and print this shot. Mount both sizes of picture, and repeat the process to make six to twelve sets of pictures.

Show one large picture to the group and talk about who is pictured. Ask the children to name the individual. Then, point to the feet of the pictured person and ask whose shoes are pictured. Have the children answer in the possessive form. Then show the group the small shoe card that matches this picture. Say, *Yes, these are _____'s shoes.*

Repeat with the other picture sets.

Extensions

Small-Group Activities

Tell the children to take off their shoes and to put them into a container. Ask the first volunteer to choose a shoe and to try to guess whose shoe it is. With the group, chant, *Whose shoe is it?* Help the child respond, *I think this is _____'s shoe.* When the owner is located, that child is the next to choose a shoe from the container.

Independent Explorations

Put the large pictures of individuals on a pocket chart and the individual footwear cards in a container nearby. The child is to select individual cards and match the shoes to the owner, saying the sentence before putting the card into the pocket.

One-on-One Instruction

Receptive Language: Lay out the full-body pictures of the class. Describe one of the pairs of shoes, asking the child to identify whose footwear it is. For example, say, *I see a pair of black gym shoes with long white laces. Whose shoes are those?*

Expressive Language: Lay out the full-body pictures in this set. Hand each child one of the small shoe pictures and ask, *Whose shoes are these?* Have the child answer in words and then match the pictures.

Family Involvement

Encourage the family to have their young child help with household chores that require identification of ownership. For example, the child might help a parent sort laundry, identifying different pieces of clothing by using possessives correctly.

I'M THINKING OF . . .

Skill

Language: descriptive words

Objectives

1. To listen to verbal descriptions

2. To identify people or objects by verbal descriptions

Description

Take random photographs of children engaged in classroom activities, classroom visitors, and people encountered on school trips. Place four photographs into a letter-sized page layout program and print them. Cut out these pictures and mount them.

Place the pictures into a pocket chart or display them along a chalkboard ledge. Describe each picture in a series of sentences. Stop after each sentence to see whether the children are able to guess who is being described. For example, say,

I am thinking of someone who is a girl.

I am thinking of someone with black hair.

I am thinking of someone who is kneeling on the floor.

I am thinking of someone who is building with blocks.

Repeat the activity several times in the group with different pictures so the children understand that each descriptive sentence offers more clues to the individual's identity. Vary the activity from time to time, using common objects.

Extensions

Small-Group Activities

Assign one child to assume the role of leader, displaying the pictures, selecting an object, and describing it. Tell the others to try to guess which object the leader is describing. The child who guesses the object or person first is then the next leader.

Independent Explorations

Tape-record descriptions to accompany each set of pictures. Put the pictures and the cassette into a labeled envelope near the tape player. The child may use the tape and earphones to listen to the descriptions and locate the described photographs.

One-on-One Instruction

Receptive Language: Play the game individually, structuring the clues to the child's level of language development.

Expressive Language: Play the game with the child acting as leader and giving the clues.

Family Involvement

Send home directions for playing the "I'm Thinking of . . . " game with the child. Stress to parents the importance of making the descriptions clear and of giving their child time to think of the answer. It helps when first beginning to play this game to limit the range of possibilities. For example, parents might play this game while waiting in line at the grocery store: *I'm thinking of something that is in our cart. It is _____.*

ON YOUR MARK, GET SET, NAME IT

Skill

Language: vocabulary development

Objectives

1. To increase vocabulary

2. To improve rapid automatic naming

3. To categorize

4. To understand and follow directions

5. To describe functions and features of objects

Description

Choose a category related to a theme or current child interests. Ask children to name objects related to that category and list them. Have children refer to the list and then locate the objects and photograph them.

Print the pictures and mount each on a large index card. Share these photographs with the group, name what they are, discuss their uses, and describe their features. Challenge the class to name the pictures as quickly as possible.

Repeat the process with several other categories.

Extensions

Small-Group Activities

Glue one or more photographs from a category to a poster and label it. Put other photographs from that category on individual cards and laminate them. Repeat the process to make other category posters. Put out one category poster; stack the individual cards that belong in that category facedown. Have one child act as the leader, turning over the top card and naming it before other group members do. The child who names it first earns the card. The person with the most cards wins.

To make the game more challenging, put out several category posters and corresponding object cards.

Independent Explorations

The child sorts the object cards into categories by placing them next to the correct poster.

One-on-One Instruction

Receptive Language: Sit with the child. Display individual object cards. Name one card and ask the child to hand it to you. Discuss the object's use.

Expressive Language: Hold all the photographs fanned out, facing you, as if playing cards. Ask the child to pick one card from your hand, to look at it, and to name and describe it.

Family Involvement

Send a note home encouraging parents to go through categories of objects at home and to have their child name them and discuss their uses. For example, ask the parents to have their child name all the objects used to make dinner.

LANGUAGE CHECKLIST

	Baseline	Period 1	Period 2
Child: _____	_/_/_	_/_/_	_/_/_

Receptive Language

	Baseline	Period 1	Period 2
To listen carefully			
To follow directions			
To demonstrate an understanding of the meanings of words			
To act out the meanings of new words			

Expressive Language

	Baseline	Period 1	Period 2
To engage in dialogue, expressing oneself			
To expand vocabulary			
To use question words and forms correctly			
To use new vocabulary appropriately in conversation			

Action Words (Verbs)

	Baseline	Period 1	Period 2
To act out physically the meanings of verbs			
To follow directions using action words			
To identify named verbs in pictures			
To describe actions in pictures			

Position Words (Prepositions)

	Baseline	Period 1	Period 2
To place objects in named positions			
To name positions of objects			
To point to positions of objects in pictures			
To name positions of objects in pictures			
To match pictures of objects by their positions			

Descriptive Words

	Baseline	Period 1	Period 2
To identify people or objects by verbal descriptions			
To describe physical attributes of people or objects			
To explain the functions of objects			

LANGUAGE CHECKLIST

	Baseline	Period 1	Period 2
Child: _____	__/__/__	__/__/__	__/__/__

Labeling Objects

	Baseline	Period 1	Period 2
To match three-dimensional objects			
To match photographs to their objects			
To match photographed objects			
To name three-dimensional objects			
To name photographed objects			

Verb Tense

	Baseline	Period 1	Period 2
To develop an appreciation for the passage of time			
To sequence events in order of occurrence			
To use regular past tense verbs correctly			
To use irregular past tense verbs correctly			
To use present tense correctly			
To use future tense correctly			

Possessive Words

	Baseline	Period 1	Period 2
To identify the ownership of objects			
To use possessive words correctly			

Color Words

	Baseline	Period 1	Period 2
To identify objects of a particular color			
To name objects of a particular color			
To name photographs of a particular color			
To group photographs by color			

CODE:

✓ = Does Consistently

± = Does Sometimes

× = Does Rarely/Does Not Do

4

Storytelling/Drama

STORYTELLING/DRAMA INTRODUCTION

What are storytelling and drama?

"Storytelling" is the age-old process of relating a tale based on a real-life event, fantasy, or fable. Oral history has been a way to transmit the shared experiences and expectations of a culture or group of people since long before written records. "Drama" is the act of portraying a story through actions and dialogue. Long before children perform in the school play, they pretend to be daddies, doctors, or superheroes.

Why are storytelling and drama important?

Storytelling is a way to transmit knowledge from one generation to another orally. It is also a method for teachers to engage young children linguistically—embedding concepts, vocabulary, and values in an interesting tale. The storyteller spins a yarn that requires the child to use imagination and to draw mental pictures. It is a valuable tool through which to model rich language.

Young children love to pretend. They easily assume the traits of another person, an animal, or an object. Through drama, children are able to say and do things that might not be acceptable in their personal relationships or daily lives. They can be brave when they don't feel brave, be naughty when they know that's not right, and be the boss when they know they are still too young to be in charge.

Dramatic play encourages children to negotiate the plot and to determine the needed characters with other children, to decide on the direction of the action, and to determine the types of props that might be needed. Through this, children plan, listen, express, socialize, negotiate, fight, and make up.

Dramatic play is a vehicle for young children to act out their understanding of a story, either real or made-up, as well as their understanding of the world in which they live.

How are storytelling and drama learned?

Storytelling is learned by being told stories frequently and by being encouraged to tell them. Children are exposed to storytelling very early in their lives. Mothers begin this with the little tales of "Patty-Cake" and "This Little Piggy" and sing the story "Rock-a-Bye Baby." Toddlers enjoy stories about other small children and revel when the storyteller is able to put them or their namesakes into the plot. Preschoolers enjoy hearing familiar stories told and retold and often join in.

Effective storytelling with young children includes the use of actions, changes of voices, props, and motions.

How are storytelling and drama facilitated?

Once a story has been told, there are many ways to encourage its retelling. The following are a few techniques for storytelling with young children.

- Show the cover of a book that has been read to the children many times. Use it as the focal point to hold the attention of the group. Instead of reading the book, tell the story in your own words.
- Display one or more key objects from the story and feature them during the appropriate point of retelling.
- Involve a puppet in the storytelling and relate the tale through this character.
- Create flannel board or magnetic board characters from this tale.
- Make masks or headbands for the children to wear during the storytelling and have the children participate at appropriate points.
- Create motions or sounds the children can make or do to enhance the plot and to keep them involved.

The idea of dramatic representation is learned by seeing teachers and parents assume voices and act out parts of a story. It is effected by using one object to represent another or by pretending to be someone or something else. It is facilitated by providing the time and environment that support it, and it develops naturally during the preschool years.

Drama can be stimulated by providing a few simple props or costumes and by encouraging children to assume a role and to playact for a little while. Nursery rhymes are a simple place to begin. They are very short stories with simple plots, little dialogue, and identifiable characters. Children who are not acting out the story can participate by becoming members of the chorus that recites the rhyme as the action progresses.

I AM THE STORY

Skill

Storytelling and dramatic play: acting and language

Objectives

1. To recall a story that has been read or told in enough detail to act it out

2. To act out the story

3. To create needed props and costumes

4. To describe the action of the story

5. To participate in the dialogue of the story where appropriate

Description

After a familiar story has been told to the group, work with the children to assemble the props and costumes they need to act it out. Allow them to dramatize the story as it was originally told or to make up their own variations. Nursery rhymes and simple folktales make very good material for beginning dramatization. Take photographs as the drama is acted out.

Review the photos with the children and select those that most accurately depict the sequence of action. Use the photos to stimulate discussion of what is going on in each shot and where it belongs in the flow of the story. Once the group agrees on which photographs to include, mount the photos on cardboard. Attach felt or sandpaper to the back and put the picture cards into an envelope.

Show the cards to the group and demonstrate how the cards can be used on the flannel board to re-create the dramatization.

Extensions

Small-Group Activities

Explain that two or three children may work together, talking about the photographs in the envelope and deciding on the correct sequence of events. They then are to place the cards in sequence from left to right on a flannel board.

Independent Explorations

Make one set of story-retelling cards for each dramatic play episode. Label each envelope so that children are able to identify its contents. Put these envelopes near a flannel board for use during free-choice time.

One-on-One Instruction

Receptive Language: Place several photographs from the drama on the table in front of the child. Describe one of the pictures and ask the child to find it. For example, say, *Find Humpty Dumpty sitting on a wall.*

Expressive Language: Print a second set of pictures. As you work with individual children, point to a photograph and have the child describe it. Write the child's description on the page, below the photograph. Talk with the child about the picture.

Family Involvement

Make a set of story-retelling cards to send home. Place the set in a thin box that has been covered with felt and that can serve as a portable flannel board. Have the child share the story with a family member.

STORYTIME PUZZLE

Skill

Storytelling and dramatic play: interpreting and describing

Objectives

1. To act out a familiar tale

2. To recognize photographs of oneself and fellow students in costume

3. To identify photographs of props used in the reenactment

4. To describe each key picture depicting the drama

Description

After reading a story or telling a tale, encourage children to act it out. Help them think of props or costumes they need. Let them take the lead in re-creating the story, but assist them when the action stalls or when they need help with a transition. As the children depict their interpretation of the story, take photographs.

Enlarge and print key photographs. Be sure to capture each character, the main props, and dramatic interactions. Glue the pictures onto a large sheet of poster board or construction paper. Next, laminate each sheet and show it to the group. Discuss what is pictured. Then, as the children watch, cut the sheets into large puzzle-shaped

pieces. Begin with only two or three pieces per picture and increase the number as the children become more skilled at puzzle assembly. Put together the puzzle as the group looks on and tell them that they may select these puzzles during center time.

Extensions

Small-Group Activities

Show the children how to mix up the pieces, choose one, and describe what is pictured (e.g., *I see the queen's crown.*). Select subsequent pieces, describing what is pictured and then assembling the puzzle. When the puzzle is completed, the group should have covered all the main elements of the story.

Independent Explorations

Put the pieces into a large envelope. Label the envelope with pictures and words so that children can retrieve it and play with the puzzle during periods of free choice.

One-on-One Instruction

Receptive Language: Place two or more puzzle pieces in front of the child. Name one of the objects in the photographs and ask the child to point to it.

Expressive Language: Turn all the puzzle pieces facedown on the table. Challenge the child to pick one and to describe what is pictured on the other side. Once each piece has been described, the child may fit the pieces together.

Family Involvement

Send the puzzle sets home for the child to play with family members. Include on the envelope directions to the parent, asking the child to describe each picture.

THE GREAT MAGNETIC ME

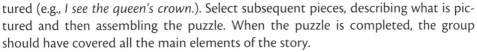

Skill

Storytelling and dramatic play: sequencing and language

Objectives

1. To use photographs mounted with magnetized tape to tell stories

2　To describe the people and events that occur in each photograph

Description

Snap photographs of a child taking part in spontaneous, imaginative, pretend play. Be sure to capture any relevant props, costumes, or scenery to enhance the quality of the photos and to stimulate story retelling.

Print the digitized photographs; then mount and back them with magnetic tape. Attach the pictures to a magnetized board.

Share the pictures with the group. Show them how to use the materials, and ask the child whose pictures are being displayed to describe what was occurring.

Extensions

Small-Group Activities

Distribute picture cards to group members at random to be organized in some order that describes their play or to create a new story.

Independent Explorations

Place the materials and the magnetic board in a center with a tape recorder. Encourage the children to insert a blank cassette tape, describe the photographs, and play back what has been said.

One-on-One Instruction

Receptive Language: Put all of the magnetized photographs on the board and play an "I'm Thinking of . . ." game. Say, *I'm thinking of,* and then describe one of the pictures in detail. Keep adding more information until the child guesses which picture is being described.

Expressive Language: Help the child use the photographs as prompts to retell the story of her or his dramatic play.

Family Involvement

Have the child take home the set of magnetized photographs, a small cassette tape player, and the tape that was recorded during independent explorations to share with parents and other family members.

CREATE A TALE

Skill

Storytelling: language and listening

Objectives

1. To create a story from real-life events

2. To expand vocabulary and verbal expressive skills

3. To listen carefully to story segments previously created in order to add meaning to them

Description

During any learning experiences, take photographs of the people, places, and things seen. Return to class and print the pictures.

Distribute the pictures to the class at random. Begin a story created by the group, in which different children describe the pictures in their possession at various times in the story. For example:

> *Once upon a time, we went on a trip to the* _____ [name the place; the child who has that picture holds it up]. *This place was very* _____ [the child describes the building]. *When we went inside, we met* _____ [name a person and have the child with that picture hold it up]. *She (or he) was a* _____, *who said, "*_____.*" Then,* . . .

Suggest to the children that they are free to volunteer any verbal description of their particular picture they choose. Tape record the story as it is being created.

Extensions

Small-Group Activities

Suggest that children look at the pictures and identify the sequence of events as they actually occurred. They then can put the photographs in that sequence.

Independent Explorations

Allow the children to play the audiotape made during group time, placing the pictures into a pocket chart in the order described in the story.

One-on-One Instruction

Receptive Language: Display all the pictures so that the child can see them and retell the story. Pause periodically, having the child locate the photograph of the person, place, or object that fits that portion of the plot.

Expressive Language: Use the same cards and the technique described for receptive language to work with a single child to elicit language. Recite the structure of a story, and each time a response is called for, encourage the child to describe the person, place, or thing in detail. Record the story so that the child can listen to it later.

Family Involvement

Send home the individual story and its audiotape created during one-on-one instruction. Include the pictures and the story outline in a packet along with directions for parents on how to use the materials. Encourage the parents to use these materials to foster verbal expression and creativity in their child. This basic exchange could be done verbally with the child in the car, while waiting to pick up a sibling, or when simply enjoying each other's company.

TELL ME A TALE

Skill

Storytelling: imagination and language

Objectives

1. To create a story based on randomly selected pictures

2. To use imagination

Description

Take a variety of photographs inside and outside the classroom. Print them and mount them on tagboard. Make sets of six to eight pictures, including in each set a location shot, some people, and some objects. Also make some tagboard strips with a descriptive term on each (e.g., strangest, most wonderful, funniest).

Tell the children they are going to look at some pictures that may not go together. Tell the children they are to use their imaginations and think up a story based on pictures they randomly select.

Some groups may need help getting started. Offer an introduction. For example:
> One day, at the _____ [find the location card], I saw the most _____ [description card] thing happen. I saw a(n) _____ [object or person card] and _____.

Extensions

Small-Group Activities

Use the same technique in a small group. Record their story and print it out to be read to the whole class later.

Independent Explorations

Some groups may need help getting started. Make a chart on poster board with blank spaces for photographs to be added during the storytelling. This can be used as the story starter. For example, place the storytelling chart and photograph cards in the activity center with a tape recorder and blank tapes. Each child may insert a blank cassette and record one or more stories.

One-on-One Instruction

Receptive Language: Display the pictures and make up a tale. As you describe each picture, pause briefly and ask the child to locate it. Then continue with the story.

Expressive Language: Begin a story and use the pictures as prompts. Encourage the child to create an appropriate description for each break in the tale. Record the story so that it can be replayed to the child later. Transcribe it on the computer and import the relevant photographs. Collect each child's stories and audiotapes so that they may be replayed and reread.

Family Involvement

Play for parents the audiotape created by their child in the one-on-one session of the story. Encourage the parents to cut out random pictures from magazines and catalogs and to challenge their child to make up a story for those pictures.

BLOCK HEADS

Skill

Dramatic play and storytelling: block play

Objectives

1. To engage in creative block play

2. To develop dramatic play skills

3. To enhance ability to create a story

Description

Make personalized blocks to build on the children's desire to play with blocks. Take a digitized photograph of each child, laminate all the photographs, and then attach each picture to a unit block. Children can then put themselves into vehicles, drive up to their block structures, get out, and enter the buildings they have created. In this process, the children have the opportunity to develop a storyline and to use their imaginations.

Extensions

Small-Group Activities

Periodically add photo blocks of people and objects that will enhance the play. For example, after a trip to the fire station, add several photo blocks of the firefighters the children have just visited.

Independent Explorations

Individuals may choose to play alone, selecting the size and number of blocks and the personalized blocks to be included in their independent play.

One-on-One Instruction

Receptive Language: Work on position words and other relevant vocabulary by giving the child one of the picture blocks and a direction to follow; for example, *Walk Jennifer all around your building. Put Jason in the bedroom.*

Expressive Language: Engage in a dialogue with the child as you play together with the blocks. Encourage descriptions of movement of the photo block through the structures that have been built.

Family Involvement

Send home copies of the photographs being used for picture blocks in school. Encourage child and parents to work together to make a set of homemade blocks from quart and half-gallon milk cartons. Provide directions on how to fold in the tops of milk cartons to form blocks. The cartons may be spray painted or left in their original form. The photographs may be added to some of these blocks.

MY OWN SLIDE SHOW

Skill

Dramatic play and storytelling: teamwork and sequencing

Objectives

1. To dress in costumes

2. To work cooperatively to decide what the characters will be doing in these costumes

3. To view photographs of children in costumes and put them in some order according to the story line that has been developed

4. To add comments for each picture

Description

Put out several costumes that suggest a theme of play. These can be occupation outfits, authentic ethnic costumes, or a variety of real-life outfits and props. Have the children interested in dramatic play put on the costumes, and watch as spontaneous play occurs. Take a variety of candid photographs as the action progresses.

After the materials have been put away, process the photographs. Print them and talk with the children about what was happening in each one. Have the group sequence the pictures.

Take the group to the computer and import the digitized photographs into a slide show program. Put the pictures into the program in the sequence determined by the children. Add either text or the children's own recorded voices to the show.

Play the program for parents as they pick up their children from school.

Extensions

Small-Group Activities

Because this activity is a popular one, make it a regular activity choice for small groups.

Independent Explorations

Print two hard copies of the photographs. Glue one set onto a sheet of construction paper to make a lotto board. Glue the second set onto individual cards that will fit onto each section on the lotto board. Show the game board and how to stack the cards and turn over the top card. The children can then match the pictures.

One-on-One Instruction

Receptive Language: Use the photo cards made for the lotto game. Lay out a few pictures and describe a card. Have the child find that card and then affirm the selection in words. For example, say, *Yes, you found the picture of the fire hose.*

Expressive Language: Play the slide show with the child; make sure that any sound effects or narrative that has been created is turned off. Have the child provide the description of what is happening in each picture.

Family Involvement

Print a hard copy of the slide show and assemble it into a booklet to be sent home each night with a different child. Include a parent comment page, and ask each family to send it back with a brief comment.

WHEN I GROW UP

Skill

Storytelling: understanding occupations

Objectives

1. To engage in dramatic play

2. To explore a variety of adult roles

Description

Use digitized photographs of children to put them into a variety of real-life roles.

Take a close-up shot of each child. Then scan a variety of photographs or illustrations depicting adults in their work clothes or uniforms. Crop each child photograph into an oval shape around the child's head. Cut out this digitized picture and move it into a scanned picture of an adult in her or his work clothes or uniform so that the child's head covers the adult's face in the original picture.

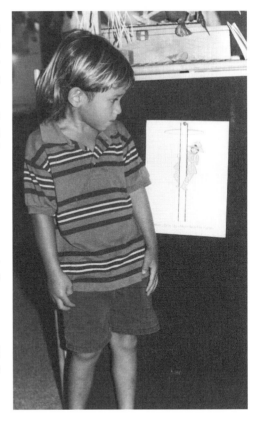

Repeat this process with each occupation being explored. Print a hard copy of each picture and assemble them into a "What I'd Like to Be" book.

Extensions

Small-Group Activities

Make a hard copy of each altered picture. Work with small groups to make occupations posters or booklets.

Independent Explorations

Let the children look through magazines and coloring books to find scenes into which they would like to have their photographs imported.

One-on-One Instruction

Receptive Language: Display the photographs of several children dressed in a variety of costumes. Describe one of the pictures and ask the child to find it; for example, *Where is the picture of James dressed as a baker?*

Expressive Language: Display the occupations posters and have the child talk about what is seen.

Family Involvement

Send home several small head shots of the child. Ask the parents and child to look through magazines, cut out pictures of workers, and glue the pictures of the child's face onto the pages. Encourage the family to talk about what the child would be doing as a grown-up involved in this occupation.

PUPPET FUN

Skill

Dramatic play and storytelling: art and acting

Objectives

1. To make simple stick puppets

2. To create a story using the puppets

Description

Take photographs of objects and people that relate to a theme or concept. Print each of these photos, and show the children how to mount them on construction paper, and then attach each one to a craft stick.

Once the stick puppets are complete, have the group work cooperatively to create a spontaneous plot.

Videotape some of these story lines. All the actors will enjoy seeing their "opening night" over and over again.

Extensions

Small-Group Activities

Put sets of theme-related puppets the children have made into clear plastic bags. Display the puppets in the dramatic play area and encourage small groups to use them to develop their own little dramas.

Independent Explorations

Provide candid photographs and miscellaneous magazines for children to cut apart to create individualized puppets. Encourage storytelling and dramatization.

One-on-One Instruction

Receptive Language: Stick all the child-made stick puppets into a large block of Styrofoam. Have the child sit facing the display of puppets. Name or describe one and have the child select it and demonstrate something about it. For example, if the boy selects a frog, he may frog leap.

Expressive Language: Select one puppet and have the child select one or two for herself or himself. Start a dialogue in character and encourage the child to talk through one of the puppets.

Family Involvement

Play the videotape for parents at a family event or show a short segment when they come to pick up their children at the end of the day. Send home a duplicate set of puppets for child and parents to play with briefly together.

WATCH ME

Skill

Dramatic play: identity and language

Objectives

1. To participate appropriately with props and costumes in beginning levels of dramatic play

2. To identify oneself in photographs taken during dramatic play

3. To comment verbally on pictures of oneself involved in dramatic play

Description

Toddlers and young preschoolers enjoy dramatic play topics similar to their own experiences. Involve them with real objects and costumes and encourage simple play.

They enjoy feeding the baby, being Mommy who carries the purse, being Daddy who drives the car, and pretending to talk on the telephone. Take photographs of the children as they take part in these activities.

Older preschoolers, kindergartners, and lower elementary school children like both fantasy play and more elaborate real-life reenactments. Their themes extend out of the home and into their neighborhoods and schools.

Print each of the photos and show them to the children. Have each child pick out a picture of herself or himself. Encourage the children to talk about what they see. Revisiting the experience this way reinforces the experience of the firsthand play.

Extensions

Small-Group Activities

Select one of the pictures, have one of the children describe what is happening in the picture, and then ask the whole group to pretend to do the same thing; for example, *Look. Molly is pretending to be Mommy sweeping with the broom. Let's all stand up and pretend to sweep.*

Independent Explorations

Enlarge the digitized photographs and make a photo gallery at the children's height along a wall that is accessible. Identify children who are between activities and seem to be having difficulty deciding what to do next; encourage them to go to look at a particular picture.

One-on-One Instruction

Receptive Language: Make a set of pictures of each child you will work with on a one-on-one basis. Take the pictures out one at a time and comment on each one. Then lay the pictures on the table and have the child point to each one as you describe it.

Expressive Language: Put each of the child's pictures into a mini photo album. Sit with the child and ask her to tell you about the photographs.

Family Involvement

Send the individualized photo albums home overnight with the children to share with their families. When the parents arrive at the end of the day, encourage them to sit with their child for a few minutes to look through their child's album. Have the child talk about what he was doing during playtime.

STORYTELLING/ DRAMA CHECKLIST

	Baseline	Period 1	Period 2
	__/__/__	__/__/__	__/__/__

Child: _____

	Baseline	Period 1	Period 2
To recall characters and plot of a story			
To act out a story			
To depict characters			
To use props and costumes appropriately			
To include dialogue in story reenactment			
To recognize costumed self in photographs			
To describe a scene in dramatic play photographs			
To retell a story, using dramatic play photographs			
To sequence a story, using dramatic play photographs			
To create a story from real-life events			
To create a made-up story			
To add to a story once started			
To engage in independent dramatic play			
To work cooperatively with others in dramatic play			
To explore a variety of adult roles			
To make stick puppets			
To create a story using puppets			

CODE:

✓ = Does Consistently

± = Does Sometimes

× = Does Rarely/Does Not Do

5

Emerging Literacy

EMERGING LITERACY INTRODUCTION

What is emerging literacy?

There is no one point in an individual's life when the person suddenly becomes fully literate. Reading and writing are complex tasks built on a variety of skills that evolve gradually over time.

"Emerging literacy" is the process of acquiring the foundation needed to learn how to read and write. It begins at birth and continues to the stage at which the child is able to employ basic, conventional reading and writing skills.

How does literacy "emerge"?

Literacy builds on the linguistic base of listening and speaking. Young children take in the language spoken to them and later experiment with the sounds and rhythms of that native language. These are the words they will later read and write. Development of solid receptive and expressive language is crucial to the process of becoming literate.

Recent research in emerging literacy reveals that young children do not enter kindergarten as blank slates, knowing nothing about either the reading or the writing process. They have, after all, lived in a literate culture, seeing the important people in their lives read newspapers, look up numbers in a telephone directory, consult signs, write checks, and jot down notes. These and many other everyday experiences have shown children that reading and writing are important and highly valued skills. Young children who see adults model the skills of reading and writing and who have been read to will eventually try to emulate these abilities and incorporate them into their dramatic play.

As they do with language, young children play with literacy and, along the way, develop a mental construct that helps them understand their experiences with print. A baby's first attempts to communicate come out as babble, an essential stage of language development. A young child's first attempts to write are expressed as scribble, an equally important stage in the development of both writing and drawing.

Young children explore and experiment with the materials of reading and writing. As they do with other early toys, infants hold, mouth, turn, throw, and look at their baby books to discover how these objects work.

Around the first birthday, children begin to develop an awareness that books are distinguished from their other toys, with a special purpose. They show a developing understanding of what is known as the conventions of reading by holding the book upright, looking at the pictures, and turning the pages. Preschoolers also begin to notice the logos for favorite products, environmental symbols such as stop signs, and the difference between the words "men" and "women" in public restrooms.

About the same time that appropriate book behavior begins to develop, children start to explore the wonders of pencils, chalk, crayons, and marking pens. They discover that writing is the process of leaving permanent marks. Over time, the scribble begins to take on a more letterlike quality until finally actual letters emerge.

Finally, children who have been read to frequently develop a sense of written language. They become familiar with book language and begin to incorporate these words and language structures into their own oral language and into their play. Such a child may be seen holding a teddy bear in his lap as he "reads" the words *Once upon a time . . .*

Why is emerging literacy important?

The stages of development that precede formal reading and writing are crucial to the eventual mastery of these skills. They are as vital to the literacy process as learning to sit up and to pull oneself to standing are to learning to walk. Without these fundamental skills, formal reading and writing instruction is fruitless.

Young children must learn through early exposure to reading that the printed word is talk written down, that it is permanent, and that it can be read by others at any time. They need to understand that symbols represent real objects or concepts and that these symbols convey meaning. A frequent question soon becomes, *What does it say?*

Children must also learn that reading and writing are crucial skills of life in a modern world. They benefit from seeing parents and teachers read directions to a recipe, follow instructions to a new game, or jot down a note to a friend.

How is emerging literacy facilitated?

Early literacy is stimulated by providing a print-rich environment where reading and writing are an integral part of all activities. This can be accomplished in many ways. For example:

- Make a variety of fiction and nonfiction books available and use them frequently.
- Label shelves and objects in the environment, fill the room with books, and use reference materials to look up answers to the children's questions.
- Model reading and writing throughout the day yourself and introduce literacy props when appropriate in dramatic play.
- Incorporate a writing center and stock it with materials that invite young illustrators and authors to express themselves.
- Act as a secretary when a child wants to dictate a thought and have it recorded on paper.
- Develop simple parent-child activity materials that can be sent home with a child or suggested to the parent to encourage literacy in the home.

PICTURE A WORD

Skill

Emerging literacy: reading

Objectives

1. To name a pictured object

2. To associate a pictured object with its spoken word

3. To associate a pictured object and its spoken word with the corresponding written word

4. To match three-dimensional letters with their printed form

Description

Ask individual children to pick out one to four objects they would like to capture photographically. Depending on the age and skill level of the children, either take the photographs yourself or assist the children in framing and taking the shots. (Note: Select objects whose names have eight or fewer letters.)

Set up a page layout program so that a standard 8½ x 11-inch page is divided in half horizontally. Insert one photograph into the top section and a second into the bottom.

Beneath each photograph, make a long, rectangular box. It will become the frame for individual letters that represent the name of the pictured object. Divide the frame into small boxes by inserting vertical strokes so that the number of small boxes equals the number of letters in the object's word.

Cut the page in half and mount it on construction paper. Add a frame of letters without the picture to the back, and laminate each card.

Provide a basket of plastic letters and show the class how to look for a specific letter. When you find the letter you want, place it in the frame over its matching letter and repeat the process until the word it completed. Then read the word aloud to the group.

Extensions

Small-Group Activities

To encourage cooperation, have children work in pairs to find the needed letters to form their word. Each pair may try to "beat the clock" by completing their word before the sand in an egg timer runs out.

Independent Explorations

Each child can decorate a small shoe box, write his or her name on it, and store the cards created in this "My Word Bank" box.

One-on-One Instruction

Ask the child to pick one of the words from the box and to read it to you. Then, name the letters to "spell" the word. As the child becomes more familiar with the words in the word bank, he or she turns the card over to read the side with the word only. The child can self-check by turning the card over to see the corresponding photograph.

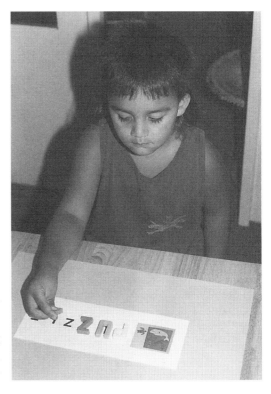

Family Involvement

Place a set of inexpensive plastic letters into the child's word bank box and secure with a rubber band. Send it home with a set of instructions for parents on how to match the letters and a note on the importance of encouraging their child's exploration of letters and sounds.

Make a parent-child activity by providing blank game cards and a computer-generated set of letter chips to be cut out. Include directions for the parent and child to look through old magazines, catalogs, or newspapers to find a picture to cut out and paste on the game board. Have the parent write the word in the letter frame, one letter per space. Then parent and child can cut out the letter cards and match them to the letters on the board.

MY FAVORITE CHARACTER

Skill

Emerging literacy: reading

Objectives

1. To understand that print is talk written down
2. To become interested in the printed word by putting oneself into the story
3. To read one's own words

Description

Have a child select a favorite book from the shelf of recently read storybooks and pick a favorite character from that book. Ask the child to tell you what she likes about that character. Record what she says.

Provide props and materials for the child to make a simple costume, mask, or headband to represent the selected character.

Take a picture of the child in the costume she has made, holding the book so that the cover is visible.

Insert the picture into a page layout program and type in the dictated words describing the favored character. Print two copies: one to be sent home and one to be put into a page protector and added to the class book.

Share the book with the class at story time and put it into the class library.

Extensions

Small-Group Activities

Have children work together to make costumes for all the characters from a book, legend, or fairy tale. Ask them to act out the story; document it with the camera. Later, print the photographs and have the children dictate or write captions to describe the story events in their own words.

Independent Explorations

Encourage children to look through well-illustrated nursery rhyme books or children's books and then to create their own props or costumes with the variety of craft materials available. Provide a child-operated tape recorder and blank tapes for children to record their own words. When a child shows such initiative, offer to capture the moment on film and to transcribe the words.

One-on-One Instruction

Read through the class book individually with the child, noting the conventions of Western reading—reading left to right, top to bottom, and from the front of the book to the back—and the written words.

Family Involvement

Send home with the child a copy of the photograph and dictated words, encouraging parents to read their child's own words. Have them share the picture and caption with friends and other family members.

Encourage parents to look through family photographs with their child and to jot down what their child says about various pictures.

"LABEL IT" BOOK

Skill

Emerging literacy: reading

Objectives

1. To label pictured objects

2. To understand the relationship between oral and written words

3. To read key words

Description

As a young child's oral vocabulary increases, introduce the idea that words can be represented in print. Decide on a category of words to be explored. Work with a small group of children, having them identify objects that belong in that category. Take a photograph of each object named.

Print each photograph taken and label it in a large, bold, easy-to-read typeface.

Create a colorful cover and add a title that reflects the subject. For example, create "My Playground" or "Things at My New School" books.

Laminate the pages and cover, stack them, and bind them into a book. Share the book with the class and then place it in the class library to be explored independently.

Variation: For classes with children from bilingual or multilingual backgrounds, write the key word in all relevant languages.

Extensions

Small-Group Activities

Divide a large project into sections, having each small group work on one part of the whole. Tell them to make a "Label It" book section for the objects included in their portion of the project. After all the sections are completed, combine them and share the finished book with the whole class.

Independent Explorations

Provide a variety of graphic material so that a child is able to cut or tear out a desired picture, glue it to paper, and then label it himself or herself, or ask to have it labeled.

One-on-One Instruction

Sit with individual children in the library corner as they go through the "Label It" book, reading the words.

Family Involvement

Have children sign out various "Label It" books created by the class to share at home.

Parent and child might look through magazines or catalogs and make their own "Label It" book. For example, in the spring, they could look through seed catalogs to pick out desired plants and then make a "Label It" book entitled "Our Garden."

PICTURE A PROJECT

Skill

Emerging literacy: reading

Objectives

1. To associate pictures with words

2. To use words and pictures in a sequence

3. To use words and pictures to complete a project successfully

Description

Identify an activity that requires a precise sequence of steps for the activity to be completed successfully (for example, making a mirror-image butterfly print). Take a photograph of each distinct step and print them all in a size that will fit on a sentence strip card. Write a brief description next to each photograph.

Place the completed sentence strips in a pocket chart.

Read each step, pointing to the words and then to the pictures before beginning the project. Tell the children that this project will be one of the options available for free choice. If they decide to do this project, they should simply follow the steps from the left side of the chart to the right side.

Extensions

Small-Group Activities

Take the strips out of the pocket chart, mix them up, and challenge a small group of children to reassemble them in the proper order by using both words and picture clues.

Independent Explorations

Develop work jobs that can be done independently, with simple directions depicted in pictures and words.

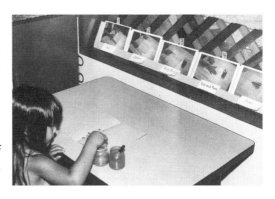

One-on-One Instruction

Ask the child to describe the sequence of directions needed for the project to be completed, using the pictures and words as cues.

Family Involvement

Develop parent-child activities with directions that can be depicted easily and quickly in pictures and words. Include the materials and the sheet of directions in a packet to be sent home.

LOOK AT WHAT WE DID

Skill

Emerging literacy: reading and writing

Objectives

1. To dictate a description of an activity

2. To read what has been written

3. To share printed words with others

Description

Have the children recall a newly completed experience or activity. This would be an appropriate follow-up to the activity "Picture a Project." Record the children's descriptions of the activity on a large language experience chart. As you write, leave space to insert one of the photographs taken of the materials or during the experience.

After the group has come to a consensus about the events, take out a glue stick and distribute the cut-out pictures randomly to the class. Reread the story and, as you come to the space, have the child who has that picture come up and glue it to the chart. Continue reading until the chart has been completed.

Fold the top of the chart over a hanger and staple it. Hang the story chart in the checkout area so that children are able to share it with their parents as they leave for the day.

Extensions

Small-Group Activities

Encourage groups of children to create their own language experience charts. When necessary, act as the secretary for the group or provide them with the spellings of words when requested.

Independent Explorations

Mount all the language experience activities on hangers and hang them at child height in a spot where children can see and read them independently.

One-on-One Instruction

Help each child make his or her own language experience pages to include in a personal journal.

Family Involvement

Type the language experience chart story and insert the digitized pictures, reduced to letter-sized format, to send home with the child.

LOOK AT ME

Skill

Emerging literacy: writing

Objectives

1. To express words and thoughts in writing

2. To see one's own words in print

3. To read one's own words to others

Description

Ask a child to identify an activity at school that he finds particularly interesting. Take a photograph of him actively engaged in that activity.

Insert the picture into a page layout program on either a half or a whole page and either with or without lines, depending on the child's writing skills.

Invite the child to either write about what he is doing in the picture or dictate the description to an adult to transcribe. After this is completed, ask the child to share it with the class at group time. Repeat for each child in the class. Suggest that those who want to share sign up for a turn in the "Author's Chair."

Extensions

Small-Group Activities

Children with common interests may choose to work on their projects together. This cooperative work requires children to communicate and negotiate to get an end product that pleases them all.

Independent Explorations

Each child can assemble his or her collection of "Look at Me" activities into a scrapbook.

One-on-One Instruction

Sit with the child as she writes; answer questions or provide written samples when asked for assistance.

Family Involvement

Place the project into a plastic page protector and send it home with the child to share with family members as a favorite activity at school.

Encourage the parent to act as a scribe when the child dictates a short piece about a favorite activity at home.

GREETING CARDS

Skill

Emerging literacy: writing

Objectives

1. To formulate thoughts to be expressed in writing

2. To observe one's own words being handwritten

3. To see one's own words in print or handwritten

Description

Take a digitized photograph of each child or of the class as a whole. Insert the photo into the front of a card-making program.

Print a card for each child, to be used as a personalized greeting card, an invitation, or a thank-you note. Encourage the children to write or dictate messages and then to sign their cards.

Group cards can be used to acknowledge a class volunteer or to thank the host of a recent field trip. Have each child sign the card and add a short message or drawing.

Record on the card the thoughts of the younger children and have them sign it.

Extensions

Small-Group Activities

Form a small committee to create a message for the greeting card to be sent from the class.

Independent Explorations

Print several copies of each card so that children have a ready supply of personalized greeting cards for their correspondence.

One-on-One Instruction

Work with each child individually to create cards for parents for holidays, birthdays, Mother's Day, Father's Day, and special events. Assist the children by writing a model of the desired word for older children or by recording the younger children's words.

Family Involvement

Ask parents to have family members send cards and letters to their young child. In return, they will need to help their child develop the habit of corresponding in response.

CATCH ME IF YOU CAN

Skill

Emerging literacy: writing

Objectives

1. To write a description of one's actions and thoughts

2. To share one's written thoughts with others

Description

Take candid photographs as the children work and play during the day. Insert each digitized photograph into a page layout program and print it. Make duplicates when more than one child is pictured.

Post the pictures in the writing center. Instruct the children to select picture sheets that feature their own pictures. Tell them to write a description of what they were doing as the picture was taken. Date the sheet and make a copy of it for the child's portfolio. Send the original home that day.

Extensions

Small-Group Activities

When several children are captured in a single photograph, have them work together to dictate an appropriate description of the activity.

Independent Explorations

Make a file of extra picture sheets printed but selected by any child. Individuals may pick a picture at random to write about, using whatever level of written expression they are currently using. Provide a date stamp so that children can easily record the date of each composition.

One-on-One Instruction

Take random photographs of the activity during the day and preview them with the child. Ask which photograph he would like printed. Encourage the child to write or dictate a description of what he was thinking, feeling, and doing as the picture was being taken.

Family Involvement

Send home one of the pictures not selected for use during the day. Ask the child to tell the parent what was going on in the picture. Suggest that the parent write the words on the sheet. Encourage the youngster to bring the completed sheet back to school to share with the class as a written project that was completed with the parent.

As a special project, the parents may give their child a disposable camera to document their time together. When the pictures are developed, the parents can encourage their child to write about what is depicted in the photographs. The child may bring these to school to share with friends.

SAMPLE WORD CARDS

Skill

Emerging literacy: writing and reading

Objectives

1. To read key words
2. To identify letters and letter sequences
3. To copy letters from a sample

Description

Emergent writers who are beginning to incorporate real letters into their writing often benefit from a model. Encourage these budding writing skills by providing a variety of blank writing cards that have pictured objects and a set of sample word cards that have the printed words completed. Laminate the sample cards, and encourage the children to look at the sample and to make their own sets of word cards.

When starting a new theme or area of interest, take some photographs of objects specific to that topic. For example, when exploring transportation, take photographs of a truck, a taxi, a train, and an ambulance.

After taking photographs of the desired objects, open a page layout program and orient it widthwise. Divide it in half to form two long cards. Then insert one digitized picture along the left-hand edge of each section. Leave ample room for the child to write the name of the pictured object. Print several copies of each sheet and cut the pages in two to form individual writing cards.

Introduce the materials at group time. Show the children the blank picture cards and the laminated sample cards with the words. Let them know that this activity is available in the writing center. They may select one of each card, find the sample, and then copy the word onto their own sheets to take home.

Extensions

Small-Group Activities

Work with a small group to identify key words for an upcoming theme or unit. Have the group select the objects to be photographed for the new word cards. Depending on the skill and maturity level of the group, have them help take the photos. Then let this group of children be the first to try out the new set of completed cards.

Independent Explorations

Provide some cards without pictures and a variety of old magazines and catalogs. The child can cut out desired pictures, glue them in place, and then write the words independently. Date and save some of these efforts to add to the child's portfolio, comparing them with ones made from a model.

One-on-One Instruction

Sit with one or two children briefly each day in the writing center as they work on their word cards. Observe their progress and note any problems they may be having.

Family Involvement

Send home some blank cards and a laminated sample to be copied at home as the parents look on.

Send home blank word cards and ask the parents to identify words meaningful to parent-child activity. Ask the parents to write a word on one blank card as their child watches and then have the child copy it. The child may bring these special word cards to school to share with the class.

PERSONALIZED SHAPE BOOKS

Skill

Emerging literacy: writing

Objectives

1. To express thoughts in writing

2. To experiment with written language

3. To collect written thoughts in a booklet

Description

As the group explores a theme or project, take photographs. Print one copy of each photograph. Have the children look through the pictures and select those they would like to include in a personalized book. Then print the desired pages for each child.

Insert the selected pages into a large sheet of construction paper folded in half to form a cover. Staple along the edge. Add a precut shape that depicts the theme or topic of the pages; glue it to the front cover. For example, if the class has recently visited a farm and now has incubating chicken's eggs in class, make a cover shape of a chick that has recently pecked its way out of its shell.

Put these booklets in the writing center. Encourage children to spend time looking through their individualized materials and writing about the pictures they have chosen to include.

Extensions

Small-Group Activities

Work with a few children to make a group shape book. Have them determine the theme, select the pictures to be included, and help with making and decorating the cover and writing the individual pages.

Independent Explorations

Once a child has completed the personalized shape book, provide additional pages the child may use for independent writing. In each, the photograph will stimulate the written expression.

One-on-One Instruction

Work with individual children, helping them with their writing as requested or required. Observe each child's progress, noting anyone who regularly avoids writing activities or who seems to be having an unusual amount of difficulty with the physical skills of manipulating a pencil.

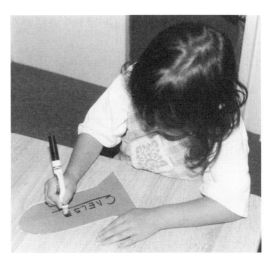

Family Involvement

Send home the finished shape book for the child to read and share with family members. Encourage parents to be supportive of their child's efforts at written expression, even when not perfect by adult standards.

EMERGING LITERACY CHECKLIST

	Baseline	Period 1	Period 2
Child: _____	_/_/_	_/_/_	_/_/_

Reading

To observe people reading			
To show an interest in symbols			
To show an interest in print			
To ask to have words identified			
To ask to have stories read			
To understand the conventions of reading (left to right, top to bottom, front to back)			
To look at books independently			
To name pictured objects			
To add pictures to a rebus			
To discuss the characters and events in books			
To contribute to a language experience story			
To match three-dimensional to printed letters			
To match letters			
To rhyme words			
To listen for sounds in words			
To match letters and sounds			
To identify written letters			
To read one's own name			
To read key words			
To read words and sentences in a book			

Writing

To watch adult writers			
To ask what an adult is writing			
To ask to be read what has been written			
To dictate words to be written by others			
To write, although not legible by others			
To copy letters			
To form identifiable letters from memory			
To copy one's own name			
To write one's own name			
To write individual words			
To express thoughts and feelings in writing			
To collect one's own writing in book form			

CODE:
✓ = Does Consistently
± = Does Sometimes
× = Does Rarely/Does Not Do

6

Social Studies

SOCIAL STUDIES INTRODUCTION

What is social studies?

"Social studies" involves the study of oneself in relationship to others and to the environment. It addresses human relationships and interdependence, from the immediate family to the global community. It explores the acquisition of social and cultural understanding through the study of current and historical topics.

Why is social studies important?

Every child is born with a unique identity, as part of a family, neighborhood, ethnic group, culture, community, country, and world. She is a social being on a quest for relevance, striving to discover how she fits into the story of life. Social studies offers opportunities to develop an understanding and appreciation of similarities and differences in people, abilities, and preferences. Moreover, it teaches children about themselves and the choices to be made in becoming productive, responsible members of a community.

How is social studies learned?

Social studies begins with nurturing experiences that help children develop self-esteem, self-direction, and self-control. As children take responsibilities for classroom chores, choose from among a variety of learning activities, and participate in cooperative projects, they begin to develop a sense belonging. Through interactions with their peers and adults in school, they learn how to develop relationships and to see themselves as a part of a group or community, outside their own families.

Children gain a growing sense of how society works by learning about their ancestors through books, art, and artifacts and through visits and personal interactions with people of various occupations, professions, and businesses. They learn about technology as they use machines, tools, and the technology. They learn about other cultures and geography as they encounter people of different ethnic groups and share stories, food, music, games, customs, and traditional dress.

How is social studies facilitated?

To make social studies relevant for young children, educators must understand the child's world and link learning with family and community values and goals. By developing activities that provide meaningful, firsthand experiences, children begin to make important connections between themselves and others. These connections can be promoted in a wide variety of ways, as outlined here.

- To foster a recognition and appreciation of human similarities and differences:
  - Take and display photographs of the children and their families.
  - Use songs and games that spotlight individual characteristics, abilities, likes, and dislikes.
  - Invite children to share experiences, thoughts, and ideas.
  - Prominently display children's work in the classroom.

- To develop an understanding of family and community roles:
  - Invite family members to visit the classroom to share life experiences, jobs, and talents.
  - Invite resource people and community helpers to visit the classroom and to talk about their work and share the tools of their trade.
  - Take children out into the community to visit stores, offices, factories, libraries, hospitals, fire stations, farms, and so on.
  - Participate in community events and celebrations.

- To develop an awareness, understanding, and appreciation of other cultures:
  - Read the children books about other peoples and cultures.
  - Invite children's family members and others to share pictures, stories, artwork, songs and dances, artifacts, clothes, and food from different ethnic groups.

o Provide a wide variety of costumes and props for integrating learning and for re-creating concepts through dramatic play.
o Have the children prepare and eat ethnic foods.

- To promote an awareness of the relationship between people and the environment:
  o Use maps and globes with the children when talking about familiar places or learning about new places.
  o Have the children plant and care for a garden that includes indigenous and foreign plants and crops.
  o Take excursions to nearby farms, gardens, forests, bodies of water, mountains, and so on.

Children gain an understanding of rights and responsibilities and learn to become vital, productive members of the classroom community when they participate in directing their learning, planning their day, and caring for themselves, others, and the classroom environment. An awareness of human interdependence will emerge if teachers embed cooperative learning throughout the curriculum and provide opportunities for direct personal experiences with others in the community.

"SHINING STARS" BOOK

Skill

Social studies: prosocial behavior

Objectives

1. To gain self-esteem

2. To participate in positive peer interactions

3. To recognize positive traits such as sharing and empathy

4. To improve communication skills

Description

Watch for prosocial behaviors from the children and take digital photographs of children engaged in those behaviors. Enlarge each photo to a 5 x 7-inch picture and print it.

Gather the children into a group and show them the photos. Invite children to identify the people pictured and to describe and discuss what is happening. Ask the children who are shown in the photos to describe their feelings. Record their comments on the paper, below the photo. Display the papers on a bulletin board.

Encourage children to look for and catch their classmates displaying a specific behavior. Explain that when they see someone _____ [e.g., helping], they should tell a teacher, who will then take a photograph of it. If the children are capable, they may take the photographs themselves.

Bind the papers together in a "Shining Stars" book.

Extensions

Small-Group Activities

Work with the children who are shown in the particular photographs. Ask both giver and receiver of the behavior to describe how the event felt to each one. Record their comments on the photograph page.

Independent Explorations

Place the "Shining Stars" book in the classroom library. Put hand-shaped blank books on the writing table and encourage children to illustrate their own stories, depicting a time when they lent a helping hand. After a child finishes her or his illustrations, the child may dictate the story.

One-on-One Instruction

Describe to the child a specific prosocial behavior. Brainstorm with him some ways the behavior might be displayed. Give the child the digital camera and explain how to operate it. Instruct him to "catch" classmates showing that behavior and to take a photograph of it. Print out the photograph and have the photographer dictate why he chose to take the photograph and what prosocial behavior it displays.

Family Involvement

Send home the "Shining Stars" book to share with parents. Invite the parents to recall specific ways their child showed this same behavior at home, to write it down, and to send it to school for their child to share with classmates.

WATCH ME GROW!

Skill

Social studies: social-emotional development and self-awareness

Objectives

1. To develop an awareness of developing abilities

2. To develop an awareness of physical growth

3. To increase self-esteem

Description

Prepare for this activity by asking parents to send several pictures of their child to school that show various stages of growth: newborn, sitting, crawling, walking, nursing or bottle feeding, parent feeding the baby, and baby feeding herself or himself.

Scan the family photographs and digitize them. Print two copies of each picture. Glue together three sheets of legal-sized paper and fold to make nine pages of an accordion-folded book.

Give the child one set of family photographs and talk about the pictures, helping the child sequence them in developmental order. Instruct the child to glue the pictures in order onto the accordion-folded pages of the book. Ask the child to describe the action; record her or his words under the picture.

Take photographs of each child, beginning with orientation to school and continuing, capturing social-emotional development for about two months.

Print two sets of photographs for each child and make an accordion book of sequential development as described above. Record children's comments about the photographs and how the children have changed as they have grown.

Extensions

Small-Group Activities

Invite two or three children to look at each other's accordion books and to comment about the growth they have seen in both their friends and themselves. Record comments about similarities and differences.

Place on the table several photographs depicting developmental milestones of each child. Describe a child at a certain developmental level. For example, say, *I am thinking of a boy who used to hold on to his mommy's legs every morning but who now just waves good-bye.*

Independent Explorations

Place the second set of photographs into a plastic bag and store in a file folder with the book. The child can sequence the set of pictures without looking at the book and then check for correctness by comparing the sequenced picture cards with the sequence in the accordion book.

One-on-One Instruction

Place the set of the child's pictures on a table. Describe an ability or preference implied by a specific photograph and ask the child to guess the photograph. For example, when looking at a photograph of the child building a block castle, say, *You used to just pile up blocks, but now you plan and build structures.*

Family Involvement

Send home the accordion book depicting the child's social-emotional development at school. Encourage the parents to read through it with their child, discussing the growth and their sense of pride in the child's accomplishments.

WHERE IN THE WORLD ARE WE?

Skill

Social studies: geography

Objectives

1. To develop geographical awareness

2. To develop an appreciation of other cultures

3. To gain an understanding of family members

Description

Take head shots of each child and input those photographs into a wallpaper page that makes multiple copies of a photograph. Cut out the small wallpaper portraits to be used as stickers with a large U.S. map attached to a wall.

Send a note home asking parents, other family members, and family friends who are planning a trip within the United States to send postcards, souvenirs, or mementos of their travels to the child.

After the child receives and examines the items, the parent should name the city and state that the items came from and help the child put them in a bag labeled with the location.

Ask the child to bring and share details about the items at school, find the location on the U.S. map, and attach one of his or her photo stickers.

Keep the map up for the entire school year, noting how many places the children have visited without leaving home.

Extensions

Small-Group Activities

Place several objects made in different countries into a cloth bag. Let the children take turns reaching into the bag and picking an object. Help the child read where the object was made and try to find the location on a world map. Encourage the children to help each other read the names of the countries and to find them on the map.

Independent Explorations

Make a classroom travel log containing the photographs described in the one-on-one activity. Use a three-ring binder to contain the pages and label a tab with each child's name. Place the binder in the class library or dramatic play area for individual children to peruse.

One-on-One Instruction

Take digital photographs of each of the souvenirs as the children bring them in. Import each photo into a page layout program, label it with the city and state of origin, and print it out. For each photograph, ask the child to explain who sent the item and something about it. Record the response on the bottom of the page. Punch holes in the paper and place it in the appropriate section of the classroom travel log.

Family Involvement

Send home a small paper bag, a line drawing of a world map, and a note asking parents to help their child find something with a label that tells where it was made (e.g., a cup labeled "Made in China"). Suggest that parents work with their child to find the country on the world map and to mark an X on the spot. Advise the parents to put the item back into the paper bag with the marked map and to send it to school with their child. At school, encourage the child to share the item during group time, show the label and name the country in which it was made, and then find the country on the classroom globe or world map.

CHEF DU JOUR

Skill

Social studies: multicultural awareness and appreciation

Objectives

1. To discover and recall the ethnic groups represented in the class

2. To taste and compare foods from different cultures

3. To hear and learn words in several languages

Description

Send notes home to parents, inviting them to come to class and prepare an ethnic recipe for a snack. Include a sign-up sheet with a choice of days and times.

When the visiting chef arrives, take a digital photograph of the person. Import the photo into a page layout program with the name of the chef, the name of the recipe, and the country in which it originated.

Take a series of four photographs as the chef prepares the food. Take another photograph of the children eating the food. Enlarge each photograph to 5 x 7 inches. Print out, seriate, and bind them together in a "Memory Book."

Share the photographs with the children during group time. Show them the photo of the chef, and read the person's name, the name of the recipe, and the country in which it originated. Locate the country on a world globe or map.

Ask the children to recall what the chef was doing in each photo; record their comments under each picture. Show the children the picture of the class eating the food; record their comments about it.

As each new chef visits the classroom to share a recipe, take photographs as described above and add them to the "Memory Book." Place the completed book in the library center for children to look at; invite parents to take turns borrowing the book.

Extensions

Small-Group Activities

Import the six photographs from each recipe (the one of the chef, the four of the preparation, and the one of the children eating) into a page layout program, making a game board with the first three pictures on the top row and the next three in the series on the bottom. Print two copies of the layout. Cut one layout into individual pieces, mount them on card stock, and laminate. Mount the game board on card stock and laminate. Invite children to choose a game board. Place the individual cards facedown on the table and play a game using lotto rules.

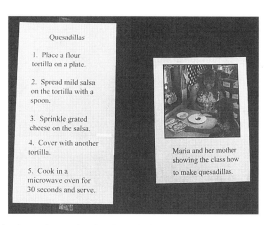

Quesadillas

1. Place a flour tortilla on a plate.

2. Spread mild salsa on the tortilla with a spoon.

3. Sprinkle grated cheese on the salsa.

4. Cover with another tortilla.

5. Cook in a microwave oven for 30 seconds and serve.

Maria and her mother showing the class how to make quesadillas.

Independent Explorations

Print out another set of game boards. Cut out the individual photographs and glue them onto index cards. Place them on a tray on a table so that children can sort the cards into ethnic recipes.

One-on-One Instruction

Make recipe charts and invite the child to help prepare a specific recipe as a snack, recalling the country of origin and family member who shared it with the class.

Family Involvement

Send home a set of picture cards from a recipe with a note instructing parents to help their child glue the cards to a sheet of paper, in order of occurrence. Suggest that the parents ask their child to describe the sequence of action taking place in each photo and then record their child's responses.

FACE THE FEELING

Skill

Social studies: emotions

Objectives

1. To identify the four basic emotions: happy, sad, angry, scared

2. To relate feelings to facial expressions

3. To become aware of the physical manifestations of emotions

Description

Discuss feelings and what situations elicit specific feelings. Sing "If You're Happy and You Know It," using facial expressions for happy, sad, angry, and scared. Take a digital head shot of each child expressing happiness and then sadness. Print a copy of each.

Cut or have children cut two 3-inch circles from tagboard. Glue the two circles together, sandwiching a craft stick between them. The result should look like a paddle.

Instruct the children to cut around their two head shots. Then have them glue the photograph showing a happy face to one side of the paddle and the sad face to the other side.

Invite the children to bring their emotions paddles to group time and to place them on the floor in front of them. Describe a scenario and ask a child to show you how it makes her feel by placing either the happy or sad photograph face up. For example, say, *You come home from school, and Mom surprises you with your favorite ice cream.*

As children progress in identifying emotions, add an angry/scared paddle. Encourage the children to use their emotions paddles to identify the feelings of characters in a story as you read it.

Extensions

Small-Group Activities

Make an emotions lotto game by importing the head shots of the children into a page layout program. Make four different lotto boards with three pictures on the top row and three on the bottom row. Make sure each board has pictures in a different order. Print out a second set of lotto boards, cutting the pictures apart and mounting them on card stock. Children can play emotions lotto by taking turns picking the top card from a stack and placing it over the matching picture.

Independent Explorations

Tape-record yourself reading common statements with different emotions (e.g., *I'm mad*). Pause between each reading. Children can play the tape and use emotions paddles to show how they think the speaker feels.

One-on-One Instruction

Ask the child to choose a book to read. Tell the child that as you read the book aloud, he should use the emotions paddles depicting happy, sad, angry, and scared to show you how the characters in the book feel at specific times. Pause and talk about the reasons for the child's conclusion.

Family Involvement

Print out on individual pages a second set of head shots for each child depicting happy, sad, angry, and scared. Send the four pages home with instructions for parents to talk with their child about each picture and what things make the child feel that way. Request that the parents record on the page what the child says and send it to school for the child to share.

MAPMAKERS

Skill

Social studies: geographical awareness

Objectives

1. To develop spatial awareness

2. To identify structures and landmarks in relation to the physical environment

3. To develop basic map-reading skills

Description

Take digital photographs of doors, windows, furniture, fixtures, and large equipment in the classroom. Print copies. Cut out the objects from the pictures and laminate them, and glue a piece of felt to the back of each object picture. Cover a bulletin board with flannel fabric and use yarn to form the basic shape of the classroom.

During group time, give each child a felt-backed picture. Ask, *Who has a door?* Invite the children with the door pictures to come up and position the pictures on the classroom outline; give guidance when necessary. Ask for the windows next, proceeding in the same manner. Ask the children, one at a time, to identify their item, locate it in the classroom, and attach it to the corresponding place on the classroom map.

Take photographs of structures, landmarks, and plants on the playground and repeat the process described above to create a playground map.

Extensions

Small-Group Activities

Place the set of felt-backed pictures of classroom items on a tray by the flannel board. Encourage small groups of children to work together to affix the items pictured to the correct place on the classroom outline, creating a map.

Independent Explorations

Place together all the felt-backed pictures from both the playground and the classroom. Children can sort the pictures into inside and outside items. They can choose to make either the classroom or playground map. Provide yarn for the map perimeter, and children can make the map by using the appropriate set of pictures.

One-on-One Instruction

Using the felt-backed photographs of objects, take turns with the child in designing a different room. One person gives the instructions about where to place the objects, and the other person puts the picture of each object in the place indicated. For example, say, *Place a door in the upper, left corner of the room.*

Family Involvement

Send home a note asking parents to walk through their home with their child, naming and counting the rooms. Ask the parents to draw the perimeter of the floor plan of their home and, working with their child, determine where each room and door should be located on the floor plan and then draw it in the appropriate place. Have them ask their child to name each room and write those words on the plan. Suggest that this plan can be used as an evacuation plan if arrows are drawn in that show the way out of the home in case of an emergency. Urge parents to post this plan and to practice evacuating the home.

WHAT'S IN HERE?

Skill

Social studies: community awareness

Objectives

1. To develop classification skills

2. To become aware of community stores and buildings

3. To match stores with their goods

Description

Take the children on an excursion to the center of town, to a mall, or on a walk around the neighborhood. Take photographs of the outside fronts of the buildings (including stores) and several objects commonly found inside the buildings (and stores). For the building photographs, enlarge the outside of each building to 8 x 10 inches. Print out all the photographs and laminate them.

Gather the group. Place the large pictures of the building fronts in a row across the floor, facing the children. Place the photographs of the objects into a decorative bag. Invite the children to come up in turn to pick a picture out of the bag, identify the picture, and place it under the building in which it is found.

Extensions

Small-Group Activities

Mount each large picture of the front of a building or store onto the upper part of 12-inch square poster board. Create a horizontal fold 2 inches from the bottom of the poster board to make a pocket. Place the photographs of the inside objects onto a tray. Invite small groups of children to work together to identify, sort, and put the object cards into the correct building pockets. Color-code the backs of the building pictures and their contents for self-correction.

Independent Explorations

Place the building pocket poster boards and object pictures in the learning center for individual classifying.

One-on-One Instruction

After using the photograph posters and cards, suggest classifying the contents of a building. Ask the child to recall other items she remembers seeing and write them down on individual cards. Invite the child to make an illustration for each item named and add them to the classifying game.

Family Involvement

Send home an old store advertisement supplement or coupon booklet. Ask parents to help their child cut or tear items out and to make a collage of store departments by categorizing items and gluing them onto paper.

OCCUPATION VISITATION

Skill

Social studies: community workers

Objectives

1. To learn the names of several occupations and professions

2. To match tools and uniforms with corresponding jobs

3. To recall and describe typical tasks involved in each job

Description

Invite workers from the community to visit the classroom and share their occupation or profession with the children. Ask them to come clothed in what they wear at work and to bring in tools common to their trade. Prepare them to talk with the children in an age-appropriate way, using simple, concrete language. Request that they talk about their occupation and clothes and demonstrate how their tools are used. Allow the children to examine and use the tools if safe and appropriate.

Take individual digital photographs of each worker dressed in work clothes and of any clothing accessories and work tools. Input the photograph at the top of the page in a 4 x 6-inch frame and print it.

During group time, show each picture and ask the children to recall the name of the person, the name of the occupation, and the names of the tools. Ask the children to describe the job and to tell how the worker uses each tool. Record responses on the corresponding photo pages and bind them together in a three-pronged clear-covered portfolio to make a book. Use the picture of the worker as the cover page of the book. Repeat for each worker who visits the classroom.

Extensions

Small-Group Activities

Print a second set of photographs with labels under each picture. Cut out each picture and mount on a 5 x 7-inch index card. Have each child pick a photograph of a different worker. Stack the "tools-of-the-trade cards" facedown on a table. Let the children take turns picking the top card, identifying the tool, and giving it to the class-mate with the corresponding worker picture.

Independent Explorations

Place all the worker and tool cards on a tray on the floor. The child can group the workers with their appropriate tools.

One-on-One Instruction

Gather the worker and tool picture cards. Show the child a picture of a worker and ask the child to name the occupation. Ask the child to recall the tools used in the occupation without looking at the pictures. Reveal the tool cards and let the child check to see whether he remembers them all. Ask the child to look at the tool cards and to describe how the tools are used.

Family Involvement

Send home a note asking parents to talk with their child about their jobs, describing their work schedules and responsibilities. Suggest taking their child to the workplace. Invite parents to visit the classroom to share their jobs with the children. Make photographic records of their visits.

WHO'S PLAYING?

Skill

Social studies: multicultural awareness

Objectives

1. To become aware of a variety of musical instruments from around the world

2. To match a person in ethnic dress with the corresponding musical instrument

3. To identify and name several ethnic musical instruments

4. To become aware of a variety of cultures and people

Description

Invite musicians to make individual visits to the classroom and to play an instrument for the children. Locate instruments from various cultures. Tape-record the music.

Take three digital photographs of each visit: one of the musician playing the instrument, one of the musician alone, and one of the instrument alone. Print and mount the individual pictures on 4 x 6-inch index cards and laminate them.

Have the children listen to a piece of taped music and find the picture of the musical instrument being played. Pause the tape and name the instrument. Have the children identify the picture of the person playing the instrument and place the instrument and player pictures side by side. Continue playing the music and having children find the corresponding instrument and person.

After the children have matched all the instruments with the musicians, check for accuracy by showing the group the picture of the musician playing the instrument.

Extensions

Small-Group Activities

Put musical instruments and items of ethnic clothing in a learning center for children to explore. Take digital photographs of children wearing costumes and playing instruments. Print the pictures and display them in the learning center.

At the snack center, display a photo of a musician playing an instrument. Provide an ethnic snack from the instrument's country of origin.

Independent Explorations

Place a variety of materials for making musical instruments in the art center. Include small boxes, rubber bands, cups, beans, tape, oatmeal boxes, empty toilet paper rolls, and so on. Children can make rhythm and stringed instruments.

One-on-One Instruction

Play a guessing game with the child. Place all the instrument and musician picture cards face up on a table. Describe an instrument or musician. For example, say, *I'm thinking of an instrument that has four strings and comes from Hawaii.* Ask the child to point to the correct picture and to name it. Take turns letting the child describe an instrument or musician.

Family Involvement

Send home a photograph of the child playing a musical instrument (see small-group activities). Instruct parents to ask their child to comment on playing the instrument and to talk about the experience. Suggest that the parents record their child's responses underneath the photograph and send it to school for their child to share with the class.

YOU MUST HAVE BEEN A BEAUTIFUL BABY

Skill

Social studies: verbal expression

Objectives

1. To match young children with their baby pictures

2. To share personal history

3. To improve verbal expressive skills

4. To build self-esteem

Description

Prepare for this activity by requesting that parents send a baby picture of their child to school. Inform them that good care will be taken of the photograph and that it will be returned the next day. Scan each picture and print and mount it. Also ask parents to write a few thoughts about their child as a baby (e.g., *On the day she was born . . .* or *The thing I remember most about him as a baby is . . .* or *The cutest thing my child ever did as a baby was . . .*).

Take a close-up photograph of each child in the class, enlarge it, and print it on letter-sized paper. Have each child select a background paper and mount the photo on the paper.

Gather the group and place a random selection of current student photographs on a display board. Chat with the group about the pictures and then pose the following: *I wonder what these children looked like when they were babies. Look at this picture. Can you guess which child this was as a baby?* Encourage children to guess who the mystery baby is. Record their predictions on a chart.

Invite the child whose baby picture it is to come up. Have the group look at the predictions on the chart to see how many children correctly guessed who this "beautiful baby" is. Read to the group the comments the parents sent about this child as a baby. Stimulate a discussion among the children about what they have seen and heard.

Extensions

Small-Group Activities

Work with two or three children to mount their pictures in an "Our Class Baby Book." Put the scanned photograph of the infant and the parents' words on one side of a magnetic page photo album. On the other side, put the child's current picture and information the child would like recorded. For example, "I am 43 inches tall and weigh 51 pounds. My favorite food is pizza. I like to draw and play at the water table."

Independent Explorations

Put several baby pictures and current pictures in the learning center for discussion and matching. Place matching color dots on the backs of the pictures to make the activity self-correcting. For example, Sara's baby picture and current photograph each have a purple dot on the back.

One-on-One Instruction

Place several current photographs of classmates on the table and describe them for the child. For example, say, *I am thinking of a child who has long red hair and who likes to play in the housekeeping center and paint at the easel.*

Print a 4 x 6-inch photograph on a letter-sized page. Show the child her baby picture and record what she says about it. Read the child's own words aloud.

Family Involvement

Send home the "Our Class Baby Book" each night with a different child. Encourage the parents to read through it with their child, discussing the different classmates and finding the child's own pages.

SOCIAL STUDIES CHECKLIST

Child: _____

	Baseline __/__/__	Period 1 __/__/__	Period 2 __/__/__

Psychology

	Baseline	Period 1	Period 2
To develop positive self-esteem			
To identify prosocial skills			
To recognize positive social traits			
To improve verbal communication			
To become aware of growth and development			
To identify basic emotions			
To understand that all people have feelings			
To understand that emotions affect people physically			
To explore one's own personal history			
To understand the relationship of self to others			

Geography

	Baseline	Period 1	Period 2
To develop geographical awareness			
To locate family and friends geographically			
To develop basic map-reading skills			
To identify structures and landmarks on a map			

Multicultural Awareness

	Baseline	Period 1	Period 2
To develop awareness of one's own culture			
To appreciate other cultures			
To explore the food, dress, and customs of other cultures			
To examine a variety of musical instruments and music			

Community Awareness

	Baseline	Period 1	Period 2
To identify buildings in the community			
To name common objects related to those buildings			
To match goods with places of business			
To name common community workers			
To match tools and uniforms to occupations			
To describe the type of work for each occupation			

CODE: ✓ = Does Consistently   ± = Does Sometimes   × = Does Rarely/Does Not Do

7

Physical Development

PHYSICAL DEVELOPMENT INTRODUCTION

What is physical development?

"Physical development "is the natural process of growth and maturation that occurs during childhood and adolescence. It includes large and small muscle skills and balance. An individual changes from a helpless infant unable to direct or control voluntary movement to a physically strong and agile teen capable of playing Mozart, sinking a 20-foot jump shot, or using tweezers to remove a splinter.

Physical skills include muscle strength, agility, control, coordination, flexibility, stamina, and balance. Physical competence is achieved when the child is able to control and care for his or her body and to perform tasks at the desired level of proficiency.

Why is physical development important?

Children explore their world through movement. Those with limited mobility because of physical disabilities are challenged in the exploration of their environment and in all the learning this investigation provides. Young children are active learners propelled by their mobility.

Reaching a motor milestone is an important achievement for both the young child and the parents. These milestones are highly visible signs of the growth and development the child is experiencing. Physical competency represents important developmental objectives during the early years and leads to a sense of achievement and self-confidence.

How is physical development learned?

Physical growth and development follow a predictable sequence, progressing gradually over time and with experience from the head and traveling downward and from the center of the body out to the extremities. Likewise, large-muscle strength and coordination precede small-muscle control. Physical development requires repeated opportunities to move, using muscles and experimenting with balance.

Physical development has its own timetable and cannot be rushed. Children need a great deal of motor practice at each stage of development to develop the muscular control and memory that are needed for the stages that follow.

How is physical development facilitated?

Large muscles develop as children are given opportunities to engage in a wide range of movement activities. Teachers should provide the equipment, space, activities, and time for children to use their muscles and to develop the subtle shifts in balance that are needed for fluid movement.

Physical skills develop primarily through play but can also be encouraged through selected teacher-directed activities. Because children enjoy physical activities and readily engage in them, it is easy to overlook those children who shy away from particular types of motor activities because they lack the skill or confidence to try them. Be sure, then, that children have ample opportunities to develop the wide range of large- and small-muscle skills. Invite reluctant children into activities, playing with them as they begin to develop skills in a new area.

Large-muscle skills include running and the use of slides, ladders, ramps, swings, balance beams, balls, sand and water table tools, tricycles, wagons, and a variety of outdoor surfaces.

Small-muscle skills are developed through the use of a wide variety of materials such as manipulative toys, blocks, puzzles, books, art materials, writing materials, clay, and rhythm instruments.

The activities presented in this chapter help children strengthen both gross and fine motor skills and cultivate the eye-hand coordination that affects perceptual and cognitive development.

ARCHITECTS UNDER CONSTRUCTION

Skill

Physical development: large muscles

Objectives

1. To increase control and balance in building with unit blocks

2. To develop visual tracking skills

3. To develop spatial awareness and perceptual motor abilities

4. To practice distinguishing foreground from background objects

5. To develop eye-hand coordination

Description

Take a photograph of a child's block structure. Transfer it to the computer and enlarge it to 5 x 7 inches. Print the photo. Label it with the child's name and description or name of the structure.

Punch ring holes in the copies and put the pages into a three-ring binder as part of a class-made book entitled "Architectural Digest." Invite children to look at the book and choose a structure to build by using the photo as a blueprint.

Extensions

Small-Group Activities

Take photographs of familiar buildings in the community and enlarge each to 8 x 10 inches. Punch ring holes in the pages and put them into a three-ring binder. Invite a few children to choose a picture of a building to construct and work together to build.

An optional activity is to take a photograph of a child's block structure, print it, and add it to the book, putting it on the page opposite the picture of the real building.

Independent Explorations

The child can draw a building and then construct it with unit blocks, using the drawing as a blueprint. Later, the teacher can take a photograph of the construction and ask the child to compare the photograph to the drawing, reflecting on his or her work.

One-on-One Instruction

In the building area of the classroom, invite the child to use wooden unit blocks to plan and construct a building with a specific number of floors. Take a photograph of the child and completed structure, and print it. Instruct the child to count and record the number of floors on the page. Add the page to the "Architectural Digest."

Family Involvement

Send home a 20-piece set of unit blocks, foam or wood. Include a note instructing the parents to build a structure with the blocks and to invite their child to copy it. Parents and child may take turns building the model and copying it.

LOOK AT WHAT I CAN DO

Skill

Physical development: large muscle coordination and spatial awareness

Objectives

1. To learn to focus attention
2. To develop balance
3. To develop an awareness of body/space relationships
4. To increase ability to reproduce specific movements accurately

Description

Take individual photographs of children performing different body movements. Enlarge the photos to at least 5 x 7 inches and print them. Cut out the pictures, mount them on construction paper, and laminate them as cards.

Place the cards facedown on the floor. Invite children to take turns being the leader, choosing a card and performing the movement shown. Then challenge the class to copy the leader's movement.

Extensions

Small-Group Activities

As an introduction to the activity, gather a small group of children. Invite a child to be the leader and to perform a body movement. Tell the leader to chant, *This is what I can do. Everybody do it too.* Tell the others to copy the leader. Take a photograph of the leader performing the movement and use it later as a transition activity.

Independent Explorations

Place the movement cards in an open area so that children can look at them and try the movements on their own.

One-on-One Instruction

To make the activity more challenging for young readers, write the name of the movement on the back of the card and ask the child to read it. After the child attempts to read it, tell the child to turn the card over to see whether he or she was correct by looking at the photo. Then tell the child to perform the movement.

Family Involvement

Send home a note asking parents to take turns performing and copying various body movements or exercises with their child.

Invite parents who know yoga positions or tai chi movements to come to class and teach them to the children. Take photographs of those parents and make a set of cards for later classroom use.

HOW DOES IT MOVE?

Skill

Physical development: large muscle coordination and locomotor skill

Objectives

1. To develop motor-planning skills

2. To use creative movement for self-expression

3. To increase motor development

4. To increase kinesthetic awareness

5. To develop motor memory

Description

During a class excursion, take digital photographs of inanimate objects that can move. For example, at the fire station you might take photographs of a fire truck, a gurney, an extension ladder, a fire hose shooting water, or a rotating flashing light. At school, print out the photographs and enlarge them to 8 x 10 inches.

As a group activity, have the children take turns choosing and identifying the object in a photograph and moving like the object in operation. Challenge the children to recall the motion verbally.

Extensions

Small-Group Activities

To make a "Creative Movement Classroom" book, take photographs of the children performing the movements of the objects. Print and put the pictures into page protectors. Place the original photo of the object into a page protector and secure it in a three-ring binder on the page opposite the photo of the children performing the motion.

Make an individual book for each excursion. Invite small groups of children to look at the book; discuss the objects and movements. Ask each child to choose a favorite movement and to form a group with other children who like that movement best. Place a line along the floor and have one child from each group stand on it. Tell the other members of each group to form a line behind their first member on the line, making a "human graph" of their favorite movements. Later, the children could record the outcome on a real graph.

Independent Explorations

Take photographs of objects in the classroom or on the playground that suggest specific movements (e.g., scissors, stapler, swing, ball, umbrella). Enlarge, print, mount, and laminate the pictures. Place them in the movement center for children to select independently. Their job is to look at a picture and then pretend their bodies are that object and move as it would, repeating for each picture.

One-on-One Instruction

Gather some objects from the classroom that suggest movement. Place them in a box. Instruct the child to choose one. Then ask the child to act out the movement of the object. Try to guess the object as the child performs, as in a game of charades.

Family Involvement

Suggest that the children take turns borrowing the "Creative Movement Classroom Book." Send home a note with the book, encouraging parents to try to perform the motions with their child or to suggest other ways to show the motions of the objects.

FOLLOW THE FLAG

Skill

Physical development: balance and figure/ground discrimination

Objectives

1. To increase spatial awareness

2. To increase awareness of directionality

3. To copy movements

4. To develop large-muscle coordination

Description

Take individual photographs of children in different positions and holding two different-colored flags. Flags can be made by taping short crepe paper strips to tongue depressors or by stapling them onto stiff cardboard strips.

Enlarge the photographs to 8 x 10 inches and print them. Mount and laminate the pictures or put them into page protectors. Secure the pages together with large book rings or in a three-ring binder. Choose one page to show to a small group of children. Give each child two flags, the same colors as in the photograph. Invite the children to copy the position, using the flags.

Extensions

Small-Group Activities

Obtain pictures of air traffic flag signals. Tell the group what the signal means and then invite one child to copy the position. Encourage other children to pretend to be airplanes obeying the flag signal. Invite children to take turns giving the signals and being the airplanes.

For more of a challenge, ask one child to choose a photograph and to give verbal directions about where to position the flags before actually performing the position for others to copy.

Independent Explorations

Place in a box on the playground the colored flags and the photographs of children holding positions. During outside play, individual children may copy the positions, using the flags.

One-on-One Instruction

Give only verbal directions for the child to follow. For example, say, *Hold the red flag in your right hand. Hold the blue flag in your left hand. Put your right hand above your head. Put your left hand straight in front of your body.*

Family Involvement

Send home two sets of blue and red flags made by the children. Include directions for the parents for taking turns with their child using the flags to create and copy positions.

DO THE LOCOMOTION

Skill

Physical development: kinesthetic awareness and position in space

Objectives

1. To practice following directions

2. To increase motor skills

3. To participate in a group

4. To practice moving in a variety of ways

5. To develop an awareness of where the body is in space

Description

Take photographs of five objects on the playground. Take photographs of children moving in five different ways, such as hopping, jumping, crawling, running, skipping, or walking backward. Enlarge the photos to at least 5 x 7 inches and print them. Mount the pictures on construction paper cards. Color-code the cards by making red dots on the backs of the object cards and black dots on the backs of the method cards. Laminate if desired.

Divide the cards into two groups: (a) the object cards (which show the destination) and (b) the method cards (which show the type of locomotion). Invite one child to choose an object card and name the destination pictured there. Invite another child to choose a method card and name the type of locomotion pictured.

Have all the children move toward the object, using the method of locomotion indicated. When all the children arrive at the destination, tell two other children to choose additional cards and to proceed in the same manner. Continue until all the children have had a chance to choose a card or until interest declines.

Extensions

Small-Group Activities

Conduct a relay race. Pick an object card. Make a starting line 15 feet away from the object indicated. Tell the children to form two relay lines behind the starting point. Pick a method card to determine how the children will move to the object. Show the children the card and have them participate in a relay race, moving as indicated to the object and returning to tap the next person in line. The first group to finish chooses the next object and method.

Independent Explorations

On the playground, mark off a track that is 4 feet wide and 15 feet long. Place method of locomotion cards in a basket at the starting line. The child can choose a card and move to the finish line in the method indicated.

One-on-One Instruction

Instruct the child to choose a locomotion card and to perform the movement in place, without moving forward. Encourage the child to try the movement again, this time moving backward.

Family Involvement

Send home a duplicate copy of the method cards and a blank set of cards. Instruct family members to help the child draw objects found outdoors near their home on the blank cards. Include directions for playing locomotion games with family members.

TACTILE MATS

Skill

Physical development: eye-hand coordination

Objectives

1. To practice spatial estimation

2. To increase small muscle control

3. To learn figure/ground discrimination

Description

Take a photograph of a familiar object and enlarge it to at least 4 x 4 inches. Print and laminate it or place it in a page protector. Place the picture on a table and invite children to replicate the object's shape by using three-dimensional material such as modeling clay or biodegradable packing material.

Show the children how to form small rolls or snakes from modeling clay and to press the pieces together to form an outline of the object. Some children may choose to fill in the whole shape itself. When using biodegradable packing material, show the children how to press one piece on a damp sponge and stick the pieces together to copy the shape.

Extensions

Small-Group Activities

Invite children to use modeling clay to make shapes or objects. Take digital photographs of the children's designs. Enlarge, print, and laminate the photos and label them with the designers' names. Place them in a box in the sensory center. Encourage children to copy their classmates' designs.

Independent Explorations

Place a wet sponge and a container of biodegradable packing material on a table in the art area for making abstract, three-dimensional structures.

One-on-One Instruction

Invite the child to use modeling clay to copy numbers or alphabet letters on laminated sheets. The child may place the modeling clay directly on the printed letter or number or form it adjacent to the pattern.

Family Involvement

Send home a 2-foot length of string or yarn in a plastic bag. Include a note asking parents to help their child form one shape or letter with the string. The next day in school, ask the child to recall and reproduce the shape made at home. Take a photograph of the string shape, print and laminate it, and use it as a pattern for classmates to use with modeling clay.

SORTING OUT THE THEMES

Skill

Physical development: small muscle control and eye-hand coordination

Objectives

1. To increase sorting skills and classification skills

2. To improve fine motor skills

3. To develop eye-hand coordination

4. To improve memory skills

Description

Take photographs of children throughout the year participating in activities that involve a particular theme. Photos may be taken on excursions or in school. Print two sets of 3 x 5-inch photos. Keep one set to make a classroom memory book of the theme and projects. Make the other set available for children to use in class.

Ask the children to cut out the pictures, spread paste on the backs, and mount them on 4 x 6-inch cards. After the paste is dry, laminate the cards. After picture cards have been made for at least two themes, invite the children to sort the pictures by thematic categories. Children may work individually or in small groups.

Extensions

Small-Group Activities

Provide a small group of children with picture cards from a specific theme. Ask them to take turns pointing to and dictating what's happening in the picture. Record each response under the photograph and ask the child to sign his or her name. On a separate card, write the name of the theme and record what the children liked about the theme. Use this card as the title page. Bind together with the photograph cards to make a memory book.

Independent Explorations

Display a theme-based memory book. Place magazines, scissors, paste, and construction paper on the table. Children can find magazine pictures that relate to or remind them of the theme. They can make a collage by cutting out the pictures and pasting them onto construction paper.

One-on-One Instruction

Place four to ten photograph cards from a recent project into a basket on a table. Invite the child to look at the cards and describe what's happening in the photograph. Ask the child to line up the cards in order of occurrence.

For a greater challenge, use number cards and invite the child to place the picture cards under the number in order of occurrence.

Family Involvement

Send home a sheet of construction paper along with a note requesting photographs from a family trip, celebration, or other event. Ask parents to let their child choose some photographs from a favorite activity and paste them onto the construction paper. Ask that the completed project be returned to school for sharing with classmates during group time.

LACE A FAVORITE

Skill

Physical development: small-muscle control and eye-hand coordination

Objectives

1. To increase spatial awareness

2. To increase directionality awareness

3. To practice decision making

4. To improve finger strength and dexterity

Description

Take photographs of children engaged in activities during the course of a day. Size the photographs to fit into the middle of a paper plate and then print the photos. Ask each of the children to choose a photograph of a favorite activity, whether they are in the picture or not.

After a child chooses a picture, direct her to glue the photograph onto a paper plate. Show the child how to punch holes around the edge of the plate, assisting as necessary. Give the child a 2-foot length of yarn, with masking tape secured around one end to make the tip stiff enough to use as a sewing needle. Instruct the child to sew around the plate by pulling the yarn either under and over, or up and down. Write or have the child write her name on the back of the paper plate and dictate what she liked about the activity captured in the photograph.

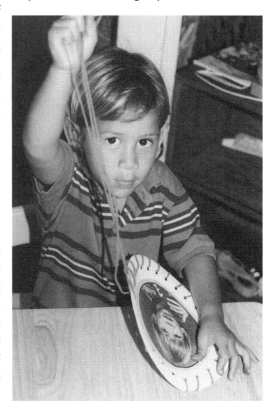

Extensions

Small-Group Activities

Take photographs from a recent excursion or project and print them. Trim the paper around each printed photo to an 8 x 9 1/2-inch square. Punch holes evenly around the edges of each photo square. Invite each child to choose a photograph. Then have the children take turns lacing their photo squares to others until a "quilt" is completed. Display the quilt in the classroom to commemorate a special event.

Independent Explorations

Arrange photographs, scissors, paper plates, glue, and a hole punch on a table. Children can make "Favorite Photo Plates" for their classmates to lace.

One-on-One Instruction

After the child has chosen a favorite picture, glue it to a rectangular piece of poster board. Punch two rows of parallel holes around the edges and give the child instructions for sewing a series of small X shapes around the picture to form a border.

Family Involvement

Send home the child's laced picture. Instruct parents to ask their child to talk about the picture and to record the child's words on the back of the paper plate. Request that they return it to school with their child for sharing at group time.

PHOTO PLACE MATS

Skill

Physical development: small-muscle control and eye-hand coordination

Objectives

1. To practice opposing motions by using scissors to cut

2. To improve tactile awareness

3. To improve motor accuracy using a pencil

4. To develop finger strength

Description

Say that the group will make personalized place mats for lunch or snack time. Ask the children to choose an object, scene, or themselves to photograph. Take a digital photograph of each child's choice. Enlarge the photos to 5 x 7 inches and print them.

Direct each child to spread glue or paste carefully on the back of the photo and then to turn the paper over and press it into the middle of a 9 x 12-inch sheet of construction paper to form a place mat. Direct the children to write their names on their construction paper place mats above their photos. Laminate the place mats and use them during lunch or snack time.

Extensions

Small-Group Activities

Invite two or three children to cut pictures out of magazines and to glue them onto a 9 x 12-inch sheet of construction paper. Instruct them to sign their names by the pictures they have chosen. Laminate or cover with clear contact paper to make a mat for use with modeling clay or during snack time.

Independent Explorations

Place glue, scissors, markers, and paper on a table in the art area with a stack of photographs and magazine pictures for exploration.

One-on-One Instruction

For more practice with fine motor skills, invite the child to use alphabet stencils with fine markers to form the letters of his or her name on a place mat.

Family Involvement

Send home a sheet of construction paper and an 18-inch length of clear contact paper. Encourage parents to look through magazines or family photographs with their child to find pictures to make a special family place mat.

SILHOUETTES

Skill

Physical development: small-muscle control and visual tracking

Objectives

1. To increase spatial awareness

2. To improve visual matching skills

3. To develop figure/ground discrimination

4. To refine eye movements

Description

Photograph an object. Transfer the photo to the computer and print it. Create a silhouette or outline of the same object by using the editing feature; print it.

Continue in the same manner for the number of desired objects until you have two sets of pictures for each object: silhouettes and colored prints.

During group time, hand out the silhouette pictures. Invite children to name the object that is silhouetted. Line up the photographs and ask one child at a time to match his or her silhouette to its corresponding picture.

Extensions

Small-Group Activities

After creating eight different silhouettes from the photographs on the computer, use the layout program to make game boards with two rows of four silhouettes each. Position the silhouettes differently for each game board. Print out the four game boards, and laminate if desired. Invite children to play a lotto game: Show them a color photograph; instruct them to find the corresponding silhouette and to place a marker over it. Continue until all silhouettes are covered.

Independent Explorations

Place a set of pictures and silhouettes on a table and invite children to match the color photographs with the silhouettes.

One-on-One Instruction

Show the child a silhouette and ask him or her to locate the real object in the classroom.

Family Involvement

Write a note home, encouraging parents to trace around kitchen utensils or common household tools on a large sheet of paper to create silhouettes and then to invite their child to match each real item with its silhouette, name the item, and discuss its use.

PHYSICAL DEVELOPMENT CHECKLIST

Child: _____

	Baseline __/__/__	Period 1 __/__/__	Period 2 __/__/__
To improve muscle strength			
To improve balance			
To improve motor control			
To develop motor-planning skills			
To develop perceptual motor skills			
To develop kinesthetic awareness			
To improve motor memory			
To increase coordination			
To reproduce movements			
To reproduce movement patterns			
To express oneself through creative movement			
To increase awareness of position in space			
To increase awareness of directionality			
To improve eye-hand coordination			
To develop figure/ground discrimination			

To develop large muscle skills:

Walking			
Running			
Hopping			
Skipping			
Jumping			
Throwing			

To develop small muscle skills:

Writing			
Tearing			
Cutting			
Pouring			
Coloring			
Painting			
Gluing			

CODE: ✓ = Does Consistently   ± = Does Sometimes   × = Does Rarely/Does Not Do

8

Mathematics

MATHEMATICS INTRODUCTION

What is mathematics?

"Mathematics" is a way of thinking that enables children to begin to organize and understand their world. It is more than just numbers and counting and rules. It arises from an attempt to solve problems with space, shapes, time, size, patterns, quantities, and relationships.

Why is mathematics important?

If mathematics is one way for children to make sense of their world, then mathematical thinking is more crucial now than ever. Children of the twenty-first century live in an information age dominated by the technology of computers, calculators, digitized data, and complicated machines. The computer affords access to a world of information that needs to be gathered, organized, analyzed, interpreted, and disseminated. Mathematics and mathematical thinking are indispensable in modern society.

How is mathematics learned?

Mathematics learning is a lengthy process that begins in infancy and continues to develop through childhood. It evolves through direct experience with real objects in play and daily life. Mathematics is learned through the rhythms of a mother's heartbeat and as infants develop patterns of eating and sleeping. They notice patterns as they begin to recognize the faces of Mom and Dad. Babies lay the foundation for spatial awareness by becoming aware of their bodies as they explore with their hands and feet. Through exploration and games like peek-a-boo, toddlers discover object constancy, a necessary concept for developing thinking and number skills. A young child starts to understand one-to-one correspondence as she counts the three candles on her birthday cake or holds up three fingers, giving each one a number.

Later, children explore shapes and colors and notice similarities and differences. While setting a table or putting away toys on a shelf, they are learning sorting and counting skills. The preschooler who completes puzzles demonstrates spatial awareness, and when he anticipates lunch, he demonstrates an awareness of time.

How is mathematical thinking facilitated?

Adults must provide opportunities for children to develop the mathematical reasoning necessary to live in today's complex, fast-paced society. Because young children learn best through hands-on experiences, mathematical concepts should be embedded in daily play and routines. Simple tasks such as using measuring cups and spoons in sand and water play, matching shoes, and putting one sock on each foot make mathematics meaningful for children. Facilitate and extend mathematical literacy by modeling the language of mathematics and by helping children name and describe their thinking and discoveries.

Provide a math-rich environment filled with opportunities to investigate relationships between materials and develop activities targeted to explore areas of mathematical learning that include the following:

- Matching
- Sorting and classifying
- Patterning
- Counting and comparing
- Exploring shapes
- Estimating
- Measuring
- One-to-one correspondence
- Geometry
- Time
- Spatial relationships
- Seriation
- Number concepts like more and less

A PLACE FOR EVERYTHING

Skill

Mathematics: sorting

Objectives

1. To group objects according to where they are used

2. To identify and organize familiar objects

3. To improve problem-solving skills

Description

Invite each child to choose an object in the classroom. Take a digital photograph of each object. Print, mount, and laminate the pictures. Place them in a gift bag. Also take a digital photograph of each learning center in the classroom. Enlarge these photographs to 8 x 10-inch prints. Mount and laminate each one.

During group time, invite each child to pick a picture from the bag, name the object, describe its use, and place it under the learning center picture where it belongs. If the child has difficulty, ask the child who originally chose the object to help. Note: This activity is particularly effective at the beginning of the school year.

Extensions

Small-Group Activities

Invite children to take turns choosing a picture, naming it, and finding the real object in the classroom.

Independent Explorations

Mount clear pockets under the pictures of the learning centers. Place a set of object cards in a basket for independent sorting into learning centers.

One-on-One Instruction

After the child has sorted the object pictures by learning centers, ask her or him to group by a different attribute. Say, *Think of another way to sort the pictures.* If the child has difficulty, suggest sorting by color, material (e.g., wood, plastic, fabric) or similar use (e.g., writing/drawing implement, reading material, building).

Family Involvement

Take photographs of children playing in the different learning centers. Print, label, mount, and laminate the pictures. Make copies of the pictures of the objects children chose and send home a sorting game with directions for use.

LOOK AT MY DAY

Skill

Mathematics: sequencing/time

Objectives

1. To gain an initial understanding of time

2. To understand the concepts of before and after

3. To recall a sequence of events

4. To use ordinal numbers

Description

Take digital photographs of children engaged in activities during the school day. Print the photos, mount them on 4 x 6-inch colored paper, and laminate them.

Gather the children and share the pictures with the group. Invite the children to choose a picture. Ask what happens first in the school day, what comes after, and so on. Using the pictures, discuss with the group the concepts of before and after.

Next, have the children come up to the front with their pictures and stand left to right, in the order the action in their pictures occurs. After they agree on the sequence, mount the pictures on cardboard. Place a clothespin as a marker next to the picture of the first event of the day and move it as children progress from one activity to another.

Extensions

Small-Group Activities

Display the chart depicting the daily sequence of events, as described earlier. Glue a picture of a clock showing the time for each activity or transition next to the photograph of it on the chart. Make copies of the clock and activity pictures. Invite children to select a clock picture, tell the time, and match it with the clock on the chart. Have them look through the activity cards and find an activity that happens at that time.

Independent Explorations

Place a set of activity cards in a box on a table adjacent to a pocket chart that has been mounted on the wall. Invite children to sequence the activity cards by placing them in order of occurrence from top to bottom.

One-on-One Instruction

Make a five-pocket chart labeled with the ordinal numbers 1st, 2nd, 3rd, 4th, and 5th. Point out the ordinal numbers to the child. Ask the child to look at the set of activity cards, to pick the activity that comes first in the day, and to put it in the corresponding pocket. Have the child continue placing the cards in order of occurrence from left to right and identifying each ordinal number in the sequence.

Family Involvement

Take photographs of other activities that are sequenced, such as hand washing, toileting, nap/rest preparation, and lunch procedures. Make sequencing game folders for children to take home and share with parents.

THE SHAPE OF THINGS

Skill

Mathematics: spatial relationships/geometry

Objectives

1. To identify and recognize shapes

2. To make shapes

3. To count the number of sides in a shape

4. To match three-dimensional shapes with their two-dimensional photographs

Description

Show the children a paper triangle. Have them count the number of sides. Then provide them with rope or sticks to make triangle shapes of their own. Have the children try to move their bodies to make the shape with their friends (show how to place three sticks to form a triangle and then invite three children to form a triangle with their bodies). Use this procedure with a variety of shapes.

Take photographs of the children forming the shapes. Print, mount, and laminate the photos. Instruct the children to match each photograph with the corresponding cutout shape. Invite children to find shapes around the room and to match each with the photograph of the children forming the shape.

Extensions

Small-Group Activities

Draw basic shapes on large cards. After the children locate objects in the room that represent these basic shapes, take photographs of them and make a sorting game. Place the picture cards facedown and invite children to take turns choosing a card and placing it on the matching shape.

Independent Explorations

Place craft sticks and a 12-inch length of rope on a tray. Place in a box the photographs of children forming various shapes. Leave these on a table in the math area. Children can use the craft sticks or rope to form the shapes in the photographs.

One-on-One Instruction

Place at least sixteen craft sticks on a tray. Ask the child to form a square with some of the sticks. If the child has difficulty, make a square with four sticks, count the four sides, and note that each side is the same length. After the child is able to form a square with four sticks, say, *Now make a bigger square, using more sticks.* Ask the child to make other shapes, increasing the challenge according to individual ability and interest.

Family Involvement

Send home a note asking parents to help their child find and identify shape objects at home and to let their child bring one object to school for sharing. Take photographs of the home objects and add them to the existing game.

EATING BY NUMBERS

Skill

Mathematics: one-to-one correspondence/matching

Objectives

1. To gain an interest in counting

2. To gain an understanding of one-to-one correspondence

3. To match shapes

Description

Over the course of several days, take a photograph of each snack available for the day. Crop the individual food items and enlarge them to actual size. Print the photos, and put them into page protectors. Place the real food items in containers on the snack table.

Remind children to wash their hands and then invite them to match the real food items to the pictured items by putting the food on top of the picture. After children have matched all the food items, they may eat the snacks and enjoy. To add interest, use food cut into different shapes to make an object corresponding to a current theme. For example, for a unit on fire safety, children can make "burnt matches" by putting pitted black olives on the tops of thin carrot sticks.

Extensions

Small-Group Activities

Invite children to make a pattern with different-shaped food items. For example, a pattern might be one cheese slice, or two apple slices. Take a photograph of the food pattern and display it for other children to copy before eating.

Independent Explorations

Provide a variety of different-shaped crackers for children to graph on laminated grids before eating them.

One-on-One Instruction

Place a variety of different-shaped cereals on a tray. Ask the child to count out a specific amount and shape to eat. (Note: Always check for food allergies before presenting any food activity.)

Family Involvement

Send home snack pictures with suggestions for parents to talk about numbers and shapes with their child as they eat.

CALL ME

Skill

Mathematics: number matching/numeral recognition

Objectives

1. To identify numerals

2. To match numerals

3. To replicate a sequence of numerals

Description

Make a class telephone book. Take a photograph of each child and teacher. Crop each photograph to a head shot measuring 3 square inches. Type the child's or teacher's name and telephone number under the photograph. Print out a page for each child and teacher. Take photographs of real or toy emergency vehicles. Type the emergency telephone number or 911 under each vehicle and print out on one page. Include this as the first page of the telephone book.

Take a photograph of the classroom telephone and mount it on construction paper to create a cover for the telephone book. Arrange the photo pages in alphabetical order by person's name and bind the pages into a classroom telephone book.

Invite the children to find their pages in the telephone book and to use a play telephone to dial their telephone numbers.

Extensions

Small-Group Activities

After receiving permission from parents, invite children to copy classmates' names and telephone numbers and to make individual telephone books to take home.

Independent Explorations

Make copies of the classroom telephone book for each child to use in dramatic play, as they pretend to call each other.

One-on-One Instruction

Give the child a telephone number and ask her to find the person it belongs to by looking in the telephone book. After she finds the correct telephone number, ask her to identify the numerals and to dial them on a play telephone.

Family Involvement

Send home the individual telephone books and ask parents to help their child identify classmates' names and telephone numbers.

COUNTING ON YOU

Skill

Mathematics: meaningful counting/numeral recognition

Objectives

1. To engage in meaningful counting

2. To learn one-to-one correspondence

3. To improve number-recognition skills

Description

Take individual photographs of children in costumes, engaged in dramatic play. Print and mount the pictures on lightweight cardboard. Cut around each body shape, and glue a felt or magnetic strip onto the back of each picture.

As the children watch, choose a felt or magnetic numeral. Place the correct number of child photographs under the numeral, using a flannel or magnetic board as appropriate.

Extensions

Small-Group Activities

Pass around a basket of felt numerals and invite each child to choose one. The children can take turns identifying the numerals and placing the correct number of photographs below the numeral on the flannel board.

Independent Explorations

Have children make number sets using pictures and erasable markers. In a basket next to a stack of vinyl place mats, place photographs of the children. Invite children to make number sets by putting photographs on a place mat, counting them, and using a marker to write the numeral on the place mat.

One-on-One Instruction

Play a sorting game with the photographs by instructing the child to sort them by gender, hair color, or eye color. Determine which group has more or less by counting and comparing the number of children in each group.

Family Involvement

Print digitized photographs of individual children, and send a set home with each child. Direct parents to help their child cut out some of the pictures and then glue one or more pictures to sheets of paper. Then the child should write the numeral of the number of pictures glued onto each sheet. To make a number book, child and parents could staple the sheets together in numerical order.

TREASURE HUNT

Skill

Mathematics: matching

Objectives

1. To improve matching skills

2. To improve visual perception skills

3. To follow directions

Description

Take photographs of items in the classroom and outside on the playground. Print them, cut out the individual items, and mount them on tagboard to make clue cards. Laminate or cover them with contact paper.

Make several treasure hunt sets, each containing three photo clue cards (either all indoor objects or all outdoor objects) and an index card divided into three sections. At each pictured object, place a self-inking stamp. Number the index card sections 1, 2, and 3. Write one of those numbers on the back of each of the clue cards. Put each set of cards into an envelope. Invite a child to choose one of the envelopes and to locate each object pictured. Tell the child to stamp the index card in the space that corresponds to the number. After all the clues have been located and the index card has been completely stamped, have the child return it to you for a treasure (e.g., sticker, stamp, other small reward).

As another activity, give an inside photo clue card to each child. Ask each child in turn to find the object pictured on her or his card. After the group has practiced a few times, give each child an outside photo clue card. Then try the treasure hunt game outdoors.

Extensions

Small-Group Activities

Conduct the treasure hunt as a small-group activity inside the classroom. To make the treasure hunt more difficult, use five picture card clues before the treasure can be found.

Independent Explorations

Make several treasure hunt sets containing three picture clue cards each. Label each clue card on the back with a number to indicate the order of the hunt. Put each set in an envelope. Children can choose an envelope and follow the numbered clues to find the treasure.

One-on-One Instruction

Ask the child to draw a picture to be used as a treasure. Instruct the child to choose three inside photo cards as clues and to make a treasure hunt game. Talk about what the first, second, and third clues will be and where to place the treasure. Suggest that the child invite a friend to play the game.

Family Involvement

Send home directions for playing the treasure hunt at home. Suggest that parents draw pictures or write words about where to find the next clue and read them to their child.

For an additional parent involvement activity, make a video of the children playing the game at school (always obtain parental permission before videotaping the children) and show it at a parent meeting. Talk about the language, mathematics, and social skills the children are learning while playing this game.

EXERCISE BY THE DAY

Skill

Mathematics: counting and concept of time

Objectives

1. To participate in counting through meaningful experience

2. To improve number-recognition skills

3. To become acquainted with the calendar and the concept of time

4. To develop large motor skills

Description

Take individual photographs of children doing a specific exercise. Resize each photo to a 3-inch square. Print and cut out the pictures. Mount six exercise photos on a 4-inch cube. (The cube can be made from two half-gallon milk cartons cut to 4 inches high. Stuff one cut-down carton with crumpled newspaper and push the other carton into it. Cover the cube with wood-grained contact paper and glue or tape a photo to each side.)

Invite children to take turns identifying the day of the month and then rolling the exercise block. The exercise photo that lands on top is the exercise of the day. Direct students to do as many of that exercise as the number of the day. For example, if the cube lands on the hopping exercise and it is May 6, the children hop six times.

Extensions

Small-Group Activities

Make a large Styrofoam die. Instruct one child to roll the die and to count the number of dots on the top side. Instruct another child to roll the exercise cube. Have all the children do the rolled number of the rolled exercise.

Independent Explorations

Put exercise cubes in a basket outside on the playground. Label the basket with a large numeral. Individual children may roll the block and perform the exercise the number of times indicated by the numeral.

One-on-One Instruction

Instruct the child to roll the exercise cube and to identify the exercise. Next, ask the child to roll a die and to count the number of dots on top. Finally, ask the child to perform the indicated number of exercises.

Family Involvement

Send home an exercise block and number card set along with instructions. Invite family members to play the exercise game with the child.

PART OF THE WHOLE

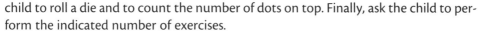

Skill

Mathematics: part to whole

Objectives

1. To improve spatial awareness in a meaningful context

2. To develop an understanding of part to whole

3. To improve problem-solving skills

4. To develop visual discrimination skills

Description

Take photographs of objects or people familiar to the children. Enlarge each of the pictures to 8 x 10 inches and print them. Remove a segment from each picture. Print a series of the pictures with an additional segment removed from each subsequent photograph.

Show a child the photo with the fewest pieces of identifying information first and ask him to guess what it is. If he is unable to do so, show the next in the series of pictures until the child is able to identify the subject.

Extensions

Small-Group Activities

Print out an additional set of complete photographs of the children in the class. Cut a rectangle approximately 1 inch from the middle of a sheet of black construction paper. Cover the photograph with the paper, positioning the cutout to reveal only the eyes of the child in the photograph. Invite children to guess the identity of the classmate. Move the rectangular window around to reveal different features until someone guesses correctly.

Independent Explorations

Cover a picture with a window template. Have the child open a window and try to guess what the picture is. Proceed with opening windows to reveal portions of the picture until the child can identify it.

One-on-One Instruction

Before the child opens a template window, ask, *What window would you like to open? What part would you like to see?* Encourage the child to name the position of the window instead of just pointing to it. Give help when necessary.

Family Involvement

Make copies of each series of pictures and put them into file folders. Attach directions for playing the game. Urge parents to work with their child, taking turns identifying the picture.

Ask parents to send a photograph to class with their child. Scan the photo and reproduce as described for use in small groups.

BIG, BIGGER, BIGGEST

Skill

Mathematics: seriation

Objectives

1. To practice comparison skills

2. To explore the concept of size

3. To develop skills in seriation

4. To improve visual discrimination

Description

Take a photograph of a familiar object. Print it. Reduce the size of the photograph by 50 percent and print it. Enlarge the original photograph by 50 percent and print it. Cover each picture with clear contact paper or laminate it.

Give a child the three pictures and ask her to put them in order. If she is unsure of what to do, ask her to arrange them from smallest to largest or vice versa. For a greater challenge, make more sizes to seriate.

Extensions

Small-Group Activities

Adjust the brightness or shade of color instead of the size of the photograph for a different type of seriation game for children to play together. Place the set of photographs on the table with a pocket chart to use for a seriation activity.

Independent Explorations

For variety, invite the children to seriate in different ways: left to right, top to bottom, biggest to smallest, smallest to biggest. Children can seriate the photographs and then explain the rationale.

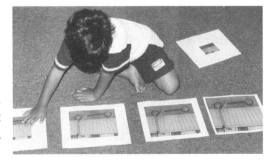

Family Involvement

Send home a note asking parents to find things at home to seriate with their child. Suggest ordering objects like measuring cups and spoons, shoes, dishes, and grades of sandpaper.

MATHEMATICS CHECKLIST

	Baseline	Period 1	Period 2
Child: _____	__/__/__	__/__/__	__/__/__

Spatial Relations and Geometry

To associate a part to its whole
To solve visual problems
To become aware of spatial relations
To match shapes
To form shapes
To count the sides of shapes
To match three-dimensional shapes with their two-dimensional pictures

Numbers and Numerals

To count by rote
To count 1 to 10 objects
To experiment with the concept of numbers
To identify numerals
To match numbers to numerals
To use ordinal numbers

Categorization

To match objects
To match one-to-one
To sort objects by one attribute
To sort objects by two or more attributes

Sequence

To copy a sequence
To recall a sequence

Seriation

To compare objects by features
To seriate objects by features

Time

To experiment with the calendar
To sequence objects and events
To associate clocks with telling time
To locate events in time (before/after)

> **CODE:**
> ✓ = Does Consistently
> ± = Does Sometimes
> × = Does Rarely/Does Not Do

9

Sensory Exploration

SENSORY EXPLORATION INTRODUCTION

What is sensory exploration?

"Sensory exploration" is the examination of people and objects in the environment through one or more of the senses. It exposes children to a range of sights, sounds, tastes, smells, and textures.

Why is sensory exploration important?

Human beings have only a few ways of getting information from the outside world into their brains for processing and storage: through the five senses and through movement. Sensory learning is a primary method of absorbing information and of learning for infants and toddlers. Language is later added to sensory experiences to help young children think and talk about the world in which they live. Preschoolers and early elementary students still rely heavily on sensory learning.

Young children need a great deal of sensory experience before they are able to identify, discriminate, understand, remember, and label sensory experiences. The information gained from this type of learning forms the basis of young children's rapidly developing cognitive world. Sensory learning literally helps children make sense out of their world.

How is sensory input processed?

The human body is one large sensory processor. It is designed to take in information from the eyes, ears, nose, mouth, and skin. Since our skin is the largest sensory organ of the human body, awareness of touch is probably the first sense the newborn experiences. The tactile sense is a primary mode of learning for the young child, providing information on size, shape, texture, and temperature.

Smell is a primitive sense. In fact, the part of the brain that processes olfactory information is sometimes referred to as "the old nose brain." Animals, including humans, are warned about impending danger, sources of food, and even potential mates through their sense of smell.

Taste is one of our most enjoyable senses. Taste buds evaluate a material's degree of sweetness, sourness, saltiness, or bitterness. These four basic taste characteristics combine to provide an almost limitless array of gustatory experiences.

Hearing begins before birth, but learning to listen is a developed skill that requires a great deal of experience. Because there is no equivalent of an eyelid over the ear, young children must learn how to listen selectively. Deciding to exclude irrelevant or less significant sounds is as important as learning to pay attention to important auditory input. The auditory sense is critical to language acquisition and later to reading development.

One of the newborn's first acts is to open his eyes, but it will take quite a long time for him to make sense out of the confusion of lines, angles, and colors that come flooding in. Over time, the child's visual acuity will develop, as will his ability to discriminate objects and to understand and recall them.

How is sensory exploration facilitated?

Because sensory learning is so important, it should be at the heart of the early childhood curriculum. Look for ways to add sensory experiences to all learning activities.

Children are bombarded with sensory input from birth, but they may need help to isolate, explore, and understand these sensations. Think of the length of time a toddler can spend opening and closing a hand around modeling clay that has had sand added to alter the texture. Children benefit from having sensory experiences isolated and emphasized as the experiences are described in words.

Fill children's environment with interesting sights, sounds, tastes, smells, and things to touch. Some school programs have learning centers devoted to sensory explorations. Other schools highlight sensory experiences through other parts of their programs. In either approach, isolate and focus on individual senses and model the vocabulary with which to discuss them. Plan ways to stimulate each of the children's senses throughout the day.

WHAT'S MISSING?

Skill

Sensory exploration: visual perception

Objectives

1. To look at a picture with a missing part, visualize the whole, and identify the person or object pictured

2. To identify the missing part of the photograph

3. To draw the missing part

Description

Take close-up photographs of various stuffed animals and dolls in the center. Place each digitized picture into a page layout program, frame it with a large box, and print it.

Next, select either the circle or the square from the tool palette. Place the cursor over one part of the picture, adjusting the size so that it covers one body part; for example, cover a teddy bear's eye. Fill the shape with the paper color so that when it is printed, this part of the picture will be omitted. Print the picture, which, for the teddy bear example, will reveal the photograph of the teddy bear missing an eye. Move the shape to cover another body part and print another picture. Repeat to make four or five pictures blocking out different body parts of the teddy bear. Laminate each picture or place each into a plastic page protector. Repeat the process for each of the stuffed animals and dolls photographed.

Show the children a whole picture and ask them to name the object pictured. Then display one of that object's altered pictures. Ask what body part is missing. Once the missing body part is named, point to the blocked portion of the picture and reaffirm the name of that body part. Repeat with the other pictures.

Let the group know that these pictures will be available in one of the centers. The group's job is to figure out what body part is missing and then to use a grease pencil or dry marker to draw it on the page.

Extensions

Small-Group Activities

Choose four to six pairs of whole and altered photographs. Place the intact pictures facedown in a row on the floor. Make a second row composed of altered pictures. Show the children how to play the game Concentration by selecting one card from the top row and one from the bottom. If the pictures match, the child keeps the cards. If not, the cards are replaced, and another child may take a turn. The goal is for the children to remember where pictures are placed once they have been seen so that

the children will be able to make a match at their next turn. The game is over when all the pairs have been located.

Independent Explorations

Place in a basket all the cards with one or more body parts covered and a photograph of one toy. Children can add the missing pieces. When they are finished, the children should erase their grease pencil markings with a small cloth and return the materials to the shelf for others to use.

One-on-One Instruction

Receptive Language: Show the child the intact picture of a stuffed animal or doll and ask the child to name it. Then show one of the cards with a missing piece. Say, *Look. Something is missing from the picture.* Point to what is missing and say, *Yes, the doll's eye is not there.*

Expressive Language: Show the child the picture of a whole animal and ask the child to name it. Then show one of the cards with a missing piece. Say, *What is missing in this picture?* Have the child name the missing part. If the child is unable to identify it, name it and ask the child to repeat it.

Family Involvement

Send home an envelope with one set of pictures, including the intact photograph and all the altered pictures. Include a grease pencil, a small wiping cloth, and directions on how parents and child can use this game together.

FUNNY FRIENDS

Skill

Sensory exploration: visual closure

Objectives

1. To scan a stack of partial pictures to form whole pictures

2. To look for visual cues

Description

Have each child in turn stand in the same spot to have a full-body photograph taken. The goal is to take a photo of approximately the same height and body proportions for each child. Mount the pictures on construction paper and laminate each one. Add a laminated title page ("Funny Friends") of construction paper. Bind the pictures together along the left side with a spiral binding. Then cut each photograph horizontally into thirds, cutting along the same spot on each page. Each third of a page may then be turned independently, creating odd combinations of pictures.

Show the children the book and have them flip through the partial pages to re-create either funny figures or the whole pictures.

Extensions

Small-Group Activities

Tell each child in a group of five to eight to dress up in a different costume from the dramatic play area. Then photograph each child so that the pictured children appear approximately the same size. Laminate, spiral-bind, and cut the pictures horizontally into thirds and then show the group their funny dress-up photographs.

Independent Explorations

Print two additional sets of photographs. Include in each set one intact photograph and one photograph cut into strips for four different children, and place each set of materials into an envelope. The children can take out the strips from one of the sets and look for clues as to the identity of the pictured child. They can use the strips as puzzle pieces to construct the whole image of the child and then use the intact photographs to self-correct.

One-on-One Instruction

Receptive Language: Use the "Funny Friends" book with the child. Flip randomly through the strips. Point to a top section and say, *I think that is _____'s head. Turn the middle and bottom sections so that we can find the other pieces to make _____'s whole body.*

Expressive Language: Show the child one of the photo strips. Ask the child to identify the classmate in the picture. Encourage the child to talk about what is visible on each strip.

Family Involvement

Make take-home puzzles of different children in the class as described in the independent explorations. Put the puzzle pieces into an envelope so that the child can take it home and reconstruct the children's photographs with family members. Encourage the parents to talk with their child about these classmates and what they do together.

SOUND LOTTO

Skill

Sensory exploration: auditory reception and memory

Objectives

1. To listen carefully to environmental sounds

2. To name the source of each sound

3. To identify the person or object that made the sound

4. To match a photograph of an object with the sound it makes

Description

Give the class the responsibility for finding ten to twelve inanimate objects in their environment that make distinctive sounds. Have the group name each object, tell how it is used, and then make the sound. Take a photograph of each object.

Make a game board by using a page layout program to orient the page lengthwise (horizontally) and to draw one horizontal line and one vertical line to make four boxes. (To make the game more challenging, add two or three vertical lines to make six or eight boxes.) Import one digitized photograph into each box. Print this page. Then create a new game board by deleting one or two pictures and importing others to fill those boxes and then printing it. Laminate each game board.

To play a lotto game, have each child select a game board. Put out buttons or other small objects for use as markers. Ask the children to look at the pictures on their boards. Place the sound-making objects behind a box top or other screen so that they are out of the sight of the children.

Shake or otherwise manipulate one of the objects to create its sound. Ask the children to identify the object that made the sound. If they have a picture of that object on their board, they should cover it with a marker. Continue with other objects; the game is over when a child has covered his or her board completely.

Extensions

Small-Group Activities

Have one child be the sound maker, moving the objects behind the screen while the other children listen for the sounds to complete their game boards.

Independent Explorations

Make a tape recording of the objects' sounds so that children can play the game independently. To make the recording, arrange the objects near a tape recorder set up with a blank tape. Be sure there is as little background noise as possible. Hold each item near the microphone and move or otherwise manipulate it for three to five seconds as it makes its distinctive sound. Let the tape run with five to eight seconds of silence before making the sound of the next object. Repeat until all of the objects have been sounded.

Show the children how to play the tape, listen to the object, and then cover its picture on a game board. Then put the setup in the listening center for individual use.

One-on-One Instruction

Receptive Language: Look at each object with the child. Talk about its distinctive features, what it does, and its name. Then ask the child to listen as you say a word and then to point to the object named.

Expressive Language: Display the objects used in the lotto game. Encourage the child to talk about each one. Ask open-ended questions that will allow the child to express thoughts about the objects at his or her level of development.

Family Involvement

Send home a cassette tape player, the sound tape, and two game boards. Include directions on how to play the game so that parents can play the game with their child.

Encourage parents to work with their child to collect objects that make distinctive sounds at home. Suggest that they hide the objects from their child's sight, manipulate each object in turn to make its sound, have the child guess what the object is, and then verify each guess by removing the object from hiding and showing it to the child.

GOING ON A TRIP

Skill

Sensory exploration: auditory sequential memory

Objectives

1. To listen to a sequence of words

2. To recall a sequence of words

Description

During a field trip or nature walk, take photographs of objects that are representative of the place being visited. For example, on a trip to a fire station, take a photograph of the building, a fire truck, a hose, a fire hydrant, a firefighter's boots, a firefighter's jacket and helmet, a hatchet, and a firefighter in uniform.

Once back in class, play a listening game with the children. Teach the children the following rhyme:

> *We went to the _____*
> *And what did we see?*
> *Here is a list*
> *As long as can be.*
> *We saw a . . .*

Ask the group to fill in the name of one of the objects they saw on the trip. Then prop up the photo of that object on the chalkboard ledge. Repeat the rhyme with the class, completing the last sentence with that word.

Name a second object and repeat the process, this time listing the two objects in order in the last sentence. Repeat with a third object. Once the group understands how to participate, turn the photo cards away from them until they have listed the objects orally. Then show the sequence to check whether they were correct.

As the children become more proficient, add to the length of the string of words that must be remembered.

Extensions

Small-Group Activities

Make a long inset board so that the photographs can be inserted quickly to create the sequence. Have one child set up the board and hold it so that the others are unable to see the pictures. Tell the leader to say the rhyme. List the words and then challenge the group to recall the sequence. Then have the leader turn the board around to show the correct answer.

Independent Explorations

Tape-record the rhyme with the string of objects named. Place the tape, a tape player, and other materials for this activity in the work area. The children can take out the photographs, insert and play the cassette tape, and then place the pictures in sequence. Make the tape self-correcting by repeating the rhyme and sequence slowly and asking the child to check.

One-on-One Instruction

Receptive Language: Lay the photographs on the table and describe one of the objects in the photos. Say, *I'm going to say two words, and I want you hand me the picture for those words in the correct order. Fire truck, boots.* The child should hand you the photos of those objects in the correct sequence. Gradually increase the number of words in the sequence.

Expressive Language: Talk with the child about the pictured objects and the experiences of the field trip. Have the child recall the events in order. Then play the memory game described in the receptive language instruction.

Family Involvement

Write out directions for this simple sequencing game so that parents can play it with their child as the family travels in the car, waits in line, or has a few moments between other activities.

TEXTURE WALK

Skill

Sensory exploration: tactile awareness

Objectives

1. To identify textures by feel alone

2. To name a variety of different textures

3. To match photographs to their real objects

Description

During group time, pass around a variety of objects that have distinctive textures. Talk about the way these items feel. Tell the group that they are going to go on a texture walk and that their job will be to find as many interesting textures as they can. Mention that each child will get to choose a textured object that you will then photograph.

Back in class, print the pictures and mount them on construction paper. Have the children talk about each texture object; write down what they say. Be sure to elicit from the children a description of the way the object feels. Bind the pages into a "Texture Book" that documents the class texture walk.

Extensions

Small-Group Activities

Work with a small group of children to arrange the object pictures into a presentation program such as PowerPoint that can be viewed on the computer. Once the sequence has been established, the children can record their voices to add a commentary for each photograph.

Independent Explorations

Print all the object pictures and place them at the work area. The children can take turns grouping the pictures by texture (e.g., rough, smooth, fuzzy).

One-on-One Instruction

Receptive Language: Place the pictures described in the independent explorations on the table. Name one texture and direct the child to find a photograph of an object that has that feel. For example, say, *Which one is sharp? . . . Yes, the knife is sharp.*

Expressive Language: Look at the "Texture Book" with the child. Ask the child to talk about what is shown on each page. Encourage a description of the texture.

Family Involvement

Show families the slide show created during the small-group activities. Encourage the families to look for different textures in their own homes and to talk about them with their children.

TOUCH A POSTER

Skill

Sensory exploration: tactile awareness

Objectives

1. To touch a variety of textures

2. To name various textures

3. To identify various textures by touch alone

4. To find objects in the environment that represent named textures

Description

Explore a variety of textures with the class over the course of several days. Each day, feature a different texture. Bring some objects of a particular texture to circle time. For example, bring a small glass mirror, a drinking glass, and a pair of eyeglasses. Name the objects and pass them around the circle. Once the children have felt the objects, name the texture. Say, *The glass feels "smooth."*

Have each child locate one object in the immediate environment that represents the texture being studied and take a photograph of it. Print the photographs and have the children paste them onto poster board to form a texture collage for each texture. Label the posters and display them in the room.

Extensions

Small-Group Activities

Import four photographs into a page layout program, with each photo representing one of the key textures being explored. Print and laminate these pictures and then cut them into individual cards. Place all the cards facedown in a basket. Have one child act as the leader, holding the basket so that another child can draw out a card and name the texture. Then, tell the small group to search the room for examples of that texture and to bring them back to the group for inspection.

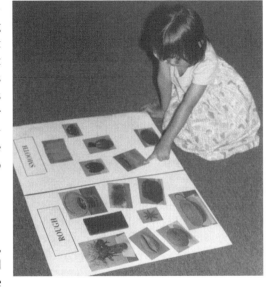

Independent Explorations

Print a second set of texture pictures, mount them on cards, and laminate. Label and glue a sample texture swatch onto a shoe box lid for each texture being explored. The children can sort the photo cards by texture into the box lids.

One-on-One Instruction

Receptive Language: Lay out two objects of different textures. Have the child feel the items. Ask the child to show you the one that represents a specific texture. For example, ask, *Which one is fuzzy?* Once the child can identify all the objects by texture, repeat with the photographs of those objects.

Expressive Language: Show a picture of an object and invite the child to tell you about it. If the child does not include a description of the texture, ask, *What does the feel like?*

Work with the child to make an individual texture book. Glue each picture onto a large index card. Ask the child to tell you about the object in the picture; write down what the child says. Have the child decorate one card as the book cover and bind the cards together into a booklet.

Family Involvement

Send home a sample of a textured object and one texture object photograph in an envelope with directions. Ask the parents to have their child identify the texture and then look around the house to find objects that match that texture. Invite the child to bring this newfound texture object to school to share with classmates.

Ask the class to find small samples of textures at home to add to the class texture posters.

SNIFF A RECIPE

Skill

Sensory exploration: olfactory awareness

Objectives

1. To match an odor with its object

2. To identify objects by smell alone

Description

Choose a recipe, such as gingerbread, that has ingredients with distinctive aromas. Take a photograph of each ingredient; print and mount the photos to make "aroma" cards. Talk with the group about making the recipe and what ingredients will be used. Show the aroma cards and name each item. Use the pictures to make a photo recipe chart.

Place each aromatic ingredient into a small container and cover with a thin piece of towel. Challenge a child to sniff one container gently and to match that smell to its picture. To verify the answer, uncover the real object. Repeat with other children and other food items.

Make the recipe. Ask the group whether any of the individual smells are still present or whether the aroma of the food is entirely new.

Extensions

Small-Group Activities

Put thin pieces of towel and the sample ingredients in their containers at a center. Have one child act as the leader, challenging other children to sniff the containers in turn and to match the smells to their pictures.

Independent Explorations

Provide three aroma cards and three sets of four containers, each with a small amount of a single food item. Children can sniff the containers and match all the smells to their aroma cards.

One-on-One Instruction

Receptive Language: Place the aroma cards on the table, facing the child. Let the child smell a lightly covered container with one of the ingredients. Ask the child to identify the picture of the object that matches that smell. Use the word as you verify the answer. For example, say, *Yes, that's the smell of cinnamon.*

Expressive Language: Show the child the aroma cards. Let the child sniff the covered ingredient; then ask the child to name the smell. For example, *That's cinnamon.*

Family Involvement

Encourage parents to include their child in cooking activities at home and to challenge their child to guess what various ingredients are by smell alone.

BY NOSE ALONE

Skill

Sensory exploration: olfactory awareness

Objectives

1. To match two containers with the same smell

2. To identify aromas by smell alone

Description

Place a cotton ball into each of several discarded film containers. Drop a different food extract (e.g., vanilla, cherry, orange, peppermint, almond, mint) or other fragrance (e.g., onion, garlic, peanut butter, perfume, aftershave) onto a separate cotton ball; cover the canisters.

Take a photograph of the real object from which each smell was extracted. Print and mount the object photos on cards.

Display the pictures. Open one of the containers and have a child take a careful whiff and then match the smell to its corresponding picture. For example, the child would match a picture of a candy cane to the peppermint smell.

Extensions

Small-Group Activities

Appoint a leader, who asks for a "sniffer" volunteer and a "blindfold" helper. Tell the helper to tie a blindfold around the sniffer's eyes. Then tell the leader to hold one of the containers under the sniffer's nose and to ask that child to name the aroma.

Independent Explorations

Place the object cards and aroma containers in the sensory learning center so that children can match smells and pictures.

One-on-One Instruction

Receptive Language: Place two or three object cards on the table and ask the child to uncap one of the containers. Have the child carefully smell the contents, match it to its picture, and name the smell.

Expressive Language: Lay each object card facedown and place its container on top of it. Have the child choose one of the containers, uncap it, and carefully smell the contents. Ask the child to name that smell. The child can self-check the answer by turning over the card.

Family Involvement

Send home a request for parents to include their young child in meal preparation, talking about the smells of the different ingredients.

MINESTRONE

Skill

Sensory exploration: gustatory awareness

Objectives

1. To taste each ingredient used to make a recipe

2. To identify items by taste alone

3. To match a pictured object with its taste

Description

Prepare to make a recipe, such as minestrone, with the children that features ingredients with distinctive tastes and textures. Have the children in turn taste each item and talk about its flavor and texture. (Use all sanitary precautions—e.g., washing hands and ingredients, using disposable tasting spoons, not sharing tasting spoons—when tasting is done in the classroom. Also check for any food allergies the children may have.)

Take a photograph of each ingredient as it is being prepared for the recipe. Cook or bake the item and take a photograph of the finished product. Have the children share in eating the final product and talking about its taste.

Afterward, print the pictures. Make a game board with two columns. Label one "Soft" and the other "Crunchy." Have the children sort the ingredient photos by texture. Some ingredients will be soft as they are added, such as cooked kidney beans, cooked macaroni, butter, precooked beef, and tomato. Other ingredients will be crunchy as they are added, such as celery, onion, and carrots.

Extensions

Small-Group Activities

Display the game board with ingredients photos. Put out a plate of other foods that are either soft or crunchy, such as peanut butter, pretzels, hard-boiled eggs, and crackers. Tell the children they may eat one of each item and describe its texture. Encourage the children to talk about their taste discoveries at this activity center. (Again, use all necessary sanitation precautions when tasting is done in the classroom.)

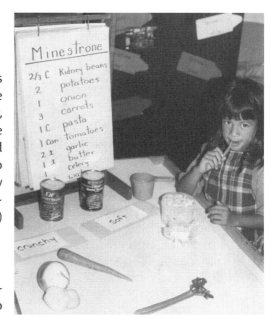

Independent Explorations

Mix up the ingredients cards in a decorative cookie tin. Children can then open it to sort the ingredients cards into categories.

One-on-One Instruction

Receptive Language: Print a copy of the photograph of each ingredient used in the recipe. Place them in front of the child and ask her to identify all the crunchy ones.

Expressive Language: Once the child has sorted the pictures in the receptive task, ask her to name each ingredient and to talk about its texture. She could say, "It's a carrot. It was hard and crunchy."

Family Involvement

Make a picture recipe card for the child to take home. The card would feature the ingredients listed by photograph, name, and quantity. Encourage parents to have their child "read" the recipe at home to different family members and to make the recipe with their child when possible.

SWEET AND SOUR

Skill

Sensory exploration: gustatory awareness

Objectives

1. To identify sweet and sour tastes

2. To identify foods that are sweet and foods that are sour

3. To identify facial expressions associated with sweet or sour foods

Description

Always remember to follow strict food preparation, health, and safety guidelines. Remind children to wash their hands before any cooking or eating activity. Also provide individual disposable tasting utensils.

Select a recipe with distinctly sweet and sour tastes, such as egg rolls with sweet and sour dipping sauce. Have the children taste the key ingredients. Take close-up photographs of individual children tasting an ingredient. On poster board, display a photograph of the object; surround it with the photos of the children tasting it. Make a separate poster for each ingredient.

Repeat with other recipes, such as lemonade, sweet and dill pickles, or pickled beets (using vinegar and sugar).

Extensions

Small-Group Activities

Put one sweet and one sour food in the activity center. Add a mirror and the "tasting" posters in the activity description. Encourage the children to look in the mirror as they taste the food and compare their facial expressions to the ones shown on the posters. (Expect lots of laughter!)

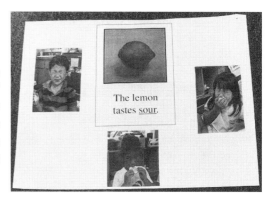

Independent Explorations

Print a set of "tasting" photographs and mount them on individual cards. Put the cards on a tray with a sweet food, a sour food, and a mirror. Children can taste the food and then find all the photos that show their classmates making a similar face when eating that particular food.

One-on-One Instruction

Receptive Language: Show two pictures: one showing a child with a pucker while tasting a sour food and another showing a child with a smile while eating something sweet. Ask the child to find the picture of a child eating something sour.

Expressive Language: Give the child a food to sample. Ask the child to name it and then to describe the taste.

Family Involvement

Let the family know that the class is exploring sweet and sour tastes. Ask the parents to talk about these tastes with their child as they prepare food. Ask that they send in a note naming and describing a sweet or a sour food their child had at home. Add these notes to the class posters.

SENSORY EXPLORATION CHECKLIST

	Baseline ___/___/___	Period 1 ___/___/___	Period 2 ___/___/___

Child: _____

Visual

To visualize the whole
To identify missing pieces of the whole
To draw the missing piece
To create a whole from various parts
To seek meaningful visual cues

Auditory

To learn to listen intently
To identify objects that make sounds
To identify the direction of a sound
To identify the person or object making a sound
To identify photographs of sources of sounds
To recall the sequence of words or sounds

Tactile

To touch various textures
To identify names of various textures
To identify textures by touch alone
To find objects that represent a named texture
To photograph objects and describe textures

Olfactory

To match an odor with its object
To identify objects by smell alone
To match containers by the smell of their contents alone
To identify odors by smell alone

Gustatory

To taste ingredients used in cooking
To identify foods by taste alone
To match a picture of an object to its taste
To identify foods as sweet or sour
To match facial expressions to tastes

CODE:
✓ = Does Consistently
± = Does Sometimes
× = Does Rarely/Does Not Do

10

Science

SCIENCE INTRODUCTION

What is science?

"Science" is the systematic study of natural phenomena. For young children, science is the exploration and discovery of the physical environment and all the living things that occupy it. Science stimulates curiosity and a sense of wonder in young children, launching them on a quest to understand the world and how it works.

The branches of science explored in this chapter are the physical and life sciences, including physics, chemistry, meteorology, general biology, botany, and zoology.

Why is science education important?

Science education is important for young children because it encourages them to think. It teaches them to ask questions and then to seek answers to the questions they have formulated.

Science experiences show children how to recognize a problem or phenomenon, form a hypothesis, experiment to test their hypothesis, organize and analyze their data, form tentative conclusions, and then evaluate their results. This process is extremely useful, not only for later science education but also as a framework for examining problems in all areas of life.

How is science learned?

Children are natural explorers. They come into the world full of curiosity and almost from their first moments are engaged in investigations, making discoveries about their bodies and their environment. Children use their senses to test important scientific concepts like gravity as they drop toast from the high chair, or cause and effect as they tug the string of a pull toy and it moves closer to them.

Science is learning by doing in its purest form. It helps children look closely, listen carefully, identify tastes, discriminate textures by touch alone, and use information gleaned from the sense of smell.

How is science learning facilitated?

The natural tendency for most adults is to answer a child's questions about the physical world with facts. Instead, to encourage scientific thinking, guide children to seek answers for themselves and put them in charge of their own investigations.

Fill their environment with materials that invite scientific exploration and stimulate thought. Change these objects frequently to keep the discovery center fresh and challenging. Offer children probing questions about the materials they are examining.

Find out what interests the children about their physical bodies or the world. Listen to their questions on these topics and tie the underlying concepts into the curriculum. Then help children find answers by structuring experiences and providing materials that afford opportunities for investigation and problem solving.

Guide children to use the scientific method. Above all, act as the model of an inquisitive adult who is herself or himself actively engaged in investigations and enthusiastic about the process.

WEIGHT FOR ME

Skill

Science: physics

Objectives

1. To learn about the force of gravity

2. To experiment with balance and weight

3. To practice meaningful counting skills

4. To improve questioning skills

Description

Gather the children into a group. Show them a small balance scale and some large and small rocks. Demonstrate how the scale works by putting a large rock on one side and adding several small rocks to the other side until the scale balances. After the children have had time to experiment with how the materials counterbalance the rock, ask the children to make predictions. Take a picture of each item to be placed on the scale. Show one card at a time and ask if the children think that that object will cause the scale to be balanced when the rock is in the other tray. Then select a child to see if the prediction was correct by putting that object into the opposing tray. Repeat until the scale balances. Then make a chart that displays the rock on one side, an equals sign, and then the combination of items that caused the scale to balance.

Next, show the children a 2-foot length of 4 x 4-inch lumber and a 6-foot length of 2 x 6-inch lumber. Ask, *Can anyone suggest how to make a balance scale from these two pieces of wood?* Wait for a response and then show them how to use the short piece of wood as a fulcrum as you center the long plank on it perpendicularly so that the plank is balanced.

Stand on one end of the plank. That end will touch the ground. Ask the class to guess how many children it will take to balance you on the scale. Invite children to stand on the other end, one at a time, until the scale balances. Explain that gravity is the invisible force that pulls on objects. Gravity is the reason why objects fall down instead of up. Gravity pulls more strongly on heavier objects. Because an adult is heavier than a child, the teacher stays down until enough children stand on the other side to add weight, thus balancing the scale.

Extensions

Small-Group Activities

In the block building area, provide long wooden planks and cylinders. Encourage children to build a balance scale and to balance it with nothing on either side of the plank. Find several sizes of blocks and let the group experiment with balancing the two sides. The gravitational pull must be the same on both sides in order to balance.

Independent Explorations

Place pennies, marbles, and other uniformly small objects in separate containers on a table with a balance scale for individual exploration and experimentation.

One-on-One Instruction

Cut a toilet paper tube in half lengthwise. Put one section, round side up, on a table along with a ruler and a bowl of pennies. Ask the child, *Can you make a balance scale with a ruler?* Invite the child to create a balance scale with the cardboard as the "fulcrum," or turning point. Instruct the child to balance the ruler on the fulcrum. Challenge the child to balance one penny on each side of the scale. Invite the child to find a small object in the room and to put it on one side of the scale and add enough pennies to the other side to balance the scale. Take a digital photograph of the balancing object and pennies. Print and record the child's exploration of the process involved in achieving the balance.

Family Involvement

Ask parents to work with their child to make a simple mobile. Suggest that they use a coat hanger, string, and assorted paper shapes with a hole punched in each. You can give them the following directions: *Tie one end of differing lengths of string to the bottom wire of the coat hanger. Tie the other end of each string through the hole in a paper shape. Hang the hanger by its hook from a knob or other object.* They can then ask their child, *Does the hanger balance?* The challenge is to make the bottom of the hanger exactly level by moving the strings with paper shapes attached along the hanger until balance is achieved.

ANIMAL TAILS

Skill

Science: zoology

Objectives

1. To identify animals by their features

2. To match animals with their tails

3. To name body parts of the animals

4. To identify body coverings: fur, feathers, skin, scales

Description

During an excursion to a farm, pet store, or zoo, take a variety of photographs of the side views of animals. Place each digitized photo into a page layout program, with the body of the animal occupying two-thirds of the page and the tail occupying the other

third of the page. Print two copies. Cut one copy of each photograph in two where the tail connects to the body.

Glue the body portion of the animal onto the front part of a paper strip. Pick up the opposite end of the paper strip and fold it in to line up with the back of the body. Crease the paper and glue the tail to the folded portion so that a whole animal is revealed.

Show children the pictures of the animals and ask them to recall the animal names. Discuss physical features and what the children remember about the animals from the excursion.

Show children the picture of an animal without its tail. Ask them to close their eyes and to visualize the tail. Instruct them to open their eyes as you fold the flap forward to reveal the tail for confirmation or correction.

Extensions

Small-Group Activities

Print out an extra copy of animal bodies and tails. Make a puzzle by laminating the picture of each animal and then cutting apart the body and the tail. Provide the group leader with the photographs of animal bodies. Distribute the animal tail pictures to the other children. Explain that the leader will hold up an animal body picture and that the child with the corresponding tail is to identify the animal and then connect the body picture and tail picture.

Independent Explorations

Place the fold-out animal body pictures on a table next to a set of animal tail pictures. Children can practice finding the tail that matches the animal body and check for accuracy by folding out the tail section of the strip.

One-on-One Instruction

Show the child only the tail picture of an animal. Have the child guess what animal it belongs to before showing the body picture. Talk about body coverings: fur (mammals), feathers (birds), skin (e.g., mammals, amphibians), scales (e.g., fish, reptiles).

Family Involvement

Send home a note asking parents to find pictures of animals in magazines. Suggest that they name the animal and discuss the physical features with their child and then use an index card to cover up a portion of an animal's body and have the child identify what animal it is.

MAGNETIC CHALLENGE

Skill

Science: magnetism

Objectives

1. To experiment with magnets, discovering items that magnets attract and do not attract

2. To use prediction skills

3. To participate in cooperative learning

Description

Magnets attract certain metals and objects that contain those metals. After children have freely explored magnets by testing objects that the magnets attract and do not attract, help them generalize their findings.

Invite children to search the classroom for small objects that they wish to test with magnets. Gather approximately fifteen of these objects, and take individual photographs of each. Print out the pictures and mount them on index cards. Laminate the picture cards and stack them together.

Bring a magnet, the objects, and the pictures to group time. Show the children an object picture card. Ask them to guess whether the magnet will attract the object pictured. After they guess yes or no, test the real object with the magnet.

Extensions

Small-Group Activities

Gather a group of three or four children. Place the real objects and a magnet in the middle of the group along with the stack of picture cards. Invite a child to draw the top card, look at the picture, and guess, by saying yes or no, whether the magnet will attract the object. If no one challenges her, she keeps the card, and the next child takes a turn. If someone challenges the guess, the challenger uses the magnet to test the real object. If correct, he keeps the card; if not, the player keeps the card. Continue playing until all cards in the stack have been used.

Independent Explorations

Place a magnet and objects on a table for exploration.

One-on-One Instruction

Supply the child with a group of objects, the object pictures, and a magnet. Make a large two-column graph with the words "Yes" and "No" at the top. Invite the child to guess whether the magnet will attract the object pictured and then to test the real object by using the magnet. Place the picture of the object on the graph in the correct column.

Family Involvement

Send home a magnet with instructions. Ask the family to encourage the child to test objects around the home to discover what the magnet will attract. Ask that parents write down what objects their child tested and the results and to return this information to school for sharing.

HEALTHFUL SNACK PARTNERS

Skill

Science: biology

Objectives

1. To learn how good nutrition promotes health

2. To identify fruits and vegetables

3. To eat fruits and vegetables

4. To participate in cooperative learning activities

Description

After exploring a unit of study on food and nutrition, discuss with the group the importance of eating at least five servings of fruits and vegetables a day. Ask the children to name their favorite fruits and vegetables.

Wash and then cut two fruits and two vegetables into bite-sized pieces. Take a photograph of an individual piece of each fruit and vegetable. Import each digitized photograph into a page layout program that duplicates the picture four times on a page. Print them out and cut them into four cards. Mount each picture on card stock and laminate. You should end up with sixteen picture cards: four for each fruit and vegetable.

Place the pictures and the cut-up fruits and vegetables on a platter on the snack table, with the picture cards in a basket. Stand wooden skewers in a cup. Invite a child to pick a snack partner; tell both partners to wash their hands. Explain that one child

will choose four to six picture cards and place them in order, left to right, on the snack table and that the partner will match the pictures with the real fruits and/or vegetables, threading them in order on a wooden skewer. Let the children reverse roles and then eat the snack.

Extensions

Small-Group Activities

Make a duplicate set of the sixteen fruit and vegetable cards. Invite two children to play a card game. Deal four cards to each child and place the rest of the stack in the middle of the table. Explain that the objective is to get as many sets of matching cards as possible. Play like the game of Go Fish, but require only two matching cards to make a set.

Independent Explorations

Place the fruit and vegetable cards on a table for sorting and patterning.

One-on-One Instruction

Begin a pattern with the fruit and vegetable picture cards. Start with a simple A-B pattern and ask the child to extend it. Proceed with more challenging patterns according to ability and interest.

Family Involvement

Send home a copy of the fruit and vegetable cards with instructions for creating and extending patterns. Suggest that parents and their child take turns creating and extending the pattern.

WHAT GROWS?

Skill

Science: botany

Objectives

1. To develop a beginning understanding of living and nonliving things

2. To discover that plants grow

3. To discover that plants need water and light to grow

4. To develop scientific thinking, using observation, prediction, and testing skills

5. To name basic parts of a plant

Description

Collect a kidney bean, penny, marble, sunflower seed, rock, and popcorn kernel.

Take a photograph of each item. Insert a photo into a page layout program, centering the photo at the top of the page. Add two columns under the photograph, one labeled "No" and the other labeled "Yes." Repeat with the other photos and print out a hard copy of each chart.

Bring the collected six items, photograph charts, six small plastic lunch bags, potting soil, and a pitcher of water to the group area. Tell the children that you want them to predict what will grow. Identify each item, place it into a bag of potting soil, and ask, *Will this _____ grow?* If a child thinks it will grow, she should sign her name in the "Yes" column under the picture; if not, she should sign under the "No" column.

After all the children have made their hypotheses, pour a small amount of water into each plastic bag and hang them from a clothesline attached to a window frame. Attach the photograph with the predictions next to the appropriate bag.

Check the bags daily for growth, ending the experiment after two weeks. Check children's predictions and actual outcomes. As the seeds sprout and grow, point out the various plant parts: roots (the first parts to emerge from the seed), stem, and leaves. Help children form conclusions about what kinds of things grow. Discuss the difference between living and nonliving things.

Extensions

Small-Group Activities

Invite each small group of children to work together in planting two lima beans. Each group should plant one of two beans in a clear plastic cup with soil and add water. One cup should be placed in a sunny place and the other in a dark place. Teams can check their beans daily for growth. Remind the children to water the beans regularly to keep them moist.

Take photographs of the planted beans every day for two weeks. Print out the photos and write the number of the day in the upper right-hand corner of the page. Ask the children to describe what they see, naming the parts of the plant. Record their responses below the pictures each day. At the end of two weeks, gather the two sets of pictures and have the children draw conclusions about sunlight and plant growth.

Independent Explorations

Invite children to help care for the school garden by planting, watering, weeding, and harvesting as needed.

One-on-One Instruction

Invite the child to find something on the playground or to bring an item from home that he thinks will grow. Provide soil, a cup, a small pitcher of water, and a marker. Ask the child to write his name and the name of the item on the cup before planting. Give the child the responsibility of caring for the plant and of watching for growth. Record results after two weeks. Ask the child to evaluate whether or not his initial hypothesis was correct.

Family Involvement

Send home a note asking parents to look around their home, yard, or neighborhood with their child to find something the child thinks might grow. Ask that they send the item to school for planting and watching for growth.

HOW'S THE WEATHER?

Skill

Science: meteorology

Objectives

1. To become aware of the weather by looking at the sky

2. To identify the characteristics of weather conditions

3. To describe and graph weather data

Description

Check the weather each morning with the children. Each day, take a photograph of the same area, which should include the sky and a tree, other plant, or wind sock.

Have the children describe the weather by looking at the picture. Ask:

What does the sky look like?

How does it feel outside?

What kind of clothes do you wear in this weather?

What can you do and what can't you do in this type of weather?

Extensions

Small-Group Activities

Make a computerized page that creates multiple copies of the same picture for each of the five types of weather (sunny, cloudy, windy, rainy, snowy) in your region. Cut them up to use on a calendar. After the children determine the weather for each day, attach the matching small photograph to the corresponding spot on the calendar. At the end of each week, have the children count and determine the most prevalent type of weather.

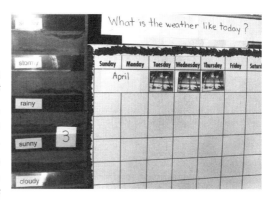

Independent Explorations

Provide page-sized graphs with pictures of the five different types of weather indicated on the vertical axis, and the number of days indicated on the horizontal axis. The children can graph the weather over a week or month by counting and recording the number of sunny, cloudy, windy, rainy, or snowy days.

One-on-One Instruction

Play a guessing game with the child. Ask the child to guess what type of weather you are thinking of. Give clues about sky conditions, temperature, appropriate dress, and activities for the weather in question.

Family Involvement

Send home a set of five weather pages, each with a picture of a different type of weather. Instruct the parents to talk with their child about the weather pictured and to ask questions such as, *What do you like about this kind of weather?* and *What can you do on this kind of day?* Suggest that family members record the child's responses and bind the pages together to make a weather book.

THE STEPS OF PLANTING

Skill

Science: botany

Objectives

1. To discover that plants are alive and grow

2. To discover that most plants have roots, stems, and leaves

3. To follow a sequence of directions

4. To develop observation skills

Description

Take photographs of the following five steps of obtaining and planting a plant slip. Make one set of these photos for each child as instructions.

1. Using a pencil to poke a hole in the potting soil

2. Using scissors to cut a stem off a potted plant

3. Dipping the cut end of the cut stem (slip) into a bowl of water

4. Dipping the cut end of the slip into rooting compound

5. Placing the slip into the previously made hole in the soil

Place the photographic instructions next to the materials needed, in order, around a table. Invite the children to follow the sequence of instructions to obtain and plant a slip.

Take a digital photograph of the child at each station. Put it into a page layout that divides the page into five equal strips horizontally. Print two copies for each child for use in the following extension activities.

Extensions

Small-Group Activities

Two or three children work together at a table, each cutting apart their own five strips depicting the planting sequence. Ask them to collaborate to create a picture story of the planting process by recalling the steps involved. Suggest that they use at least one strip from each person in the group, line them up in order from left to right, and then glue the chosen strips to a 4-foot length of 12-inch-wide butcher paper. Encourage the children to discuss the process, describing what is happening in the photographs. Record their responses below the pictures.

Independent Explorations

Put potting soil in a large plastic tub on a table in the sensory center. Place a variety of beans, some plant cuttings, and small garden tools next to the tub. Allow children to experiment with digging and planting.

One-on-One Instruction

Instruct the child to cut apart her five photographs. Mix up the photographs and have her put them in order, recalling the steps of planting. Afterward, direct the child to put the photographs in an envelope and label it with her name.

Family Involvement

Send home the five photo strips previously cut by the child at school. Include a note to the parents: Ask your child to recall the sequence of the process. Have him paste the photographs in order on a paper strip. Ask him to describe what he is doing in each picture and write his words below the pictures. Send this project back to school for sharing with the class.

RISING TO THE OCCASION

Skill

Science: chemistry

Objectives

1. To gain a beginning understanding of gases and the expansion of gases

2. To observe changes that occur in the expansion of gases

3. To gain an understanding of the three states of matter: solid, liquid, gas

Description

Conduct this introductory demonstration of inflating a balloon with baking soda and vinegar. First, let the children touch the baking soda; say, *This is baking soda. It is solid matter.* Let the children dip their fingers in vinegar. (Make sure fingers have no cuts; vinegar will make cuts sting!) Say, *This is vinegar. It is liquid matter.* Next, use a funnel to pour baking soda into a bottle that has a small opening. Then pour in some vinegar and quickly stretch the mouth of a balloon over the opening. The balloon will inflate. Ask the children what made the balloon inflate: a solid, a liquid, or a gas. Point out the bubbles in the bottle and discuss the chemical reaction that occurred when vinegar was added to the soda. The gas called carbon dioxide was given off and inflated the balloon.

Photograph each step in making a recipe for bread. Take photographs of mixing all the ingredients, including yeast, together, letting the dough rise, punching the dough down, and letting it rise again before putting the bread into the oven to bake.

Print the photographs of the bread-making process and mount them on a poster board, creating a photographic recipe. Number the steps and laminate the board. Post it in the cooking area and invite children to help make bread by following the recipe. As children notice the bread rising, make sure they look closely at the bubbles in the dough; discuss gas formation. When punching down the dough, point out the escape of gas. After cooking the bread, slice it and point out

the holes, caused by the gas, in the bread. Then let the children eat the bread.

Recall with the group the steps and the process by looking at the photographs. Discuss how the bread rose and the role of yeast in making gas.

Extensions

Small-Group Activities

Read to the group the story "The Little Red Hen" and invite children to act out the steps the hen took to get ready to make bread. Show the children the recipe pictures; ask them to identify the solids and liquids and to recall what they did. Record their responses.

Independent Explorations

Put baby food jars, spoons, baking soda, and vinegar on a discovery table. Encourage children to explore the substances and to experiment with mixing the baking soda and vinegar.

One-on-One Instruction

Resize the photographs of the bread-making recipe to 2 x 3 inches each and print them out. Instruct the child to arrange the pictures in correct order for making the recipe. Allow the child to glue the photos onto a sheet of paper to take home.

Family Involvement

Send home the child's picture recipe with a note to the parents directing them to ask their child about each step and to write her or his words under each picture, paying special attention to the pictures of the rising dough.

MAGIC CRYSTALS

Skill

Science: chemistry

Objectives

1. To notice the changes in states of matter
2. To practice prediction skills

3. To test hypotheses

4. To increase observation skills

Description

Fill a clean glass bottle with very hot tap water. Add several teaspoonfuls of sugar to the hot water and stir. Continue adding sugar and stirring until no more sugar will dissolve. Cut a length of string that is a few inches longer than the height of the bottle. Tie one end of the string to a paper clip. Tie the other end of the string around the middle of a pencil. Place the pencil across the top of the bottle, with the paper clip hanging into the bottle. Wind the string around the pencil until the paper clip hangs just above the bottom of the bottle.

Take a digital photograph of the bottle with the sugar solution and string. Print it and place it at the top of a prediction chart labeled from Day 1 through Day 5. Ask the children to guess how many days they think it will take for crystals to form; then have them sign their names under the number of days they predict.

Take a digital photograph of the bottle of sugar solution every day at the same time. Print and display the photo above the numbered day. Remind the children to look for changes and crystal formation. Guide the children to compare their predictions with the results observed and recorded in the photograph.

Extensions

Small-Group Activities

Leave the bottle of growing crystals on the table for several days after the experiment. Suggest that the children continue to observe. Record the crystal growth with digital photographs. Then take the string out of the water and place the crystals on a small dish. Invite children to examine the crystals with a magnifying lens, or place a few crystals on a microscope slide and let the children view them with a microscope.

Independent Explorations

Place sugar, salt, and sand in open containers on a table in the discovery area. Provide a magnifying lens, microscope slides, and a microscope. Invite children to examine the crystals, noting that each different substance has its own crystal shape.

One-on-One Instruction

Place the containers of sugar, salt, and sand on a table and take a digital photograph of each one. Import each photo into a page layout program, placing the photo at the top of the page. Print and label the three photographs. Ask the child to examine and describe each crystal. Record the responses on the page below the corresponding photograph.

Family Involvement

Put in an envelope for parents a 12-inch length of string, a paper clip, and directions for growing crystals as done in the initial activity description. Suggest that they add food coloring to the water as they try the activity with their child or try to grow a different type of crystal by stirring salt or washing soda into the hot water instead of sugar. Ask the parents to help their child record the growth of the crystals. Invite the child to bring the cluster of crystals to school to share with classmates.

SCIENCE TALK

Skill

Science: scientific terms

Objectives

1. To understand the meanings of scientific words

2. To act out the meanings of scientific terms

3. To use new scientific vocabulary appropriately in conversation

Description

Make scientific vocabulary meaningful to young children by first explaining the words and then acting them out. For example, when studying butterflies, expose the group to the "proboscis" through which the butterfly drinks plant nectar. Include costumes that could be as simple as headbands with pipe cleaner antennae. Give each child butterfly a party favor that unrolls when it is blown. Show the children how to fly close to the blossom of a plastic plant and then extend the proboscis to pretend to drink a drop of liquid from the flower.

Take photographs of the dramatization so that children are able to print out copies to put into their individual word banks.

Extensions

Small-Group Activities

Work with a few children at a time to make individual science word banks. For each child, print out a set of key science pictures from the lesson being studied (e.g., a caterpillar, a chrysalis, antennae, a proboscis). Have the children name and talk about each of the pictures as they cut them out and paste them onto 5 x 7-inch index cards. Print the words for the children, naming the letters as they watch the letters being formed. Bind each set of cards together by punching holes in them and securing with a book ring.

Independent Explorations

Put costumes corresponding to the new vocabulary words into the dramatic play center with a mirror and the photo cards made in the small-group activities.

One-on-One Instruction

Share the props for the new vocabulary words with the child and then look at the photographs. Name one of the new words and ask the child to find it in the picture. For example, say, *Find the proboscis on the butterfly.*

Review the photo vocabulary cards in the child's word bank, asking the child to name the objects pictured.

Family Involvement

Send home a duplicate set of some of the child's new words from the word bank. Ask the parents to sit with their child and listen to the description of the words and what was done at school to learn about them.

SCIENCE CHECKLIST

	Baseline	Period 1	Period 2
Child: _____	_/_/_	_/_/_	_/_/_

Scientific Method

To observe			
To question			
To develop predictive skills			
To test a hypothesis			
To work cooperatively in discovery			
To use scientific terms			

Zoology

To name animals			
To identify animal body parts			
To identify body coverings: fur, feathers, skin, scales			
To identify animals by their features			

Physics

To learn about the force of gravity			
To explore balance			
To experiment with a lever			

Physical Science

To experiment with magnets		
To identify materials that magnets attract		

Biology

To learn about nutrition		
To learn how good nutrition promotes health		

CODE: ✓ = Does Consistently ± = Does Sometimes × = Does Rarely/Does Not Do

---

11

Toddlers and Technology

TODDLERS AND TECHNOLOGY INTRODUCTION

What is toddlerhood?

The term "toddlerhood" is applied to the stage of development during which the child is learning to walk or "toddles," which usually occurs around the child's first birthday. This period extends through approximately three years of age and is characterized by the development of specific motor, language, cognitive, and social-emotional milestones.

Why is toddlerhood important?

Each stage of development is critical to the skills and stages that come later. Toddlerhood is characterized by the emergence of independence that accompanies new mobility, an explosion of language skills and, as Vygotsky suggested, an emerging ability to use words as "the tools for thought (Vygotsky, 1986, p. 94)." While toddlers are increasingly more socially aware and adept in their interactions with adults and other children, they are still primarily egocentric. Since toddlers are the center of their own little universes, all activities that feature them or include them in any way are of interest.

Toddlers develop imitation skills important to learning. They watch others perform daily tasks and imitate those actions and words. They are increasingly aware of the expression of emotions in others, and they exhibit a wide variety of their own feelings.

During the toddler years, there is a cognitive shift from a reliance on trial-and-error learning to a more planned approach to tasks. Their thinking about mathematical concepts develops as a way to understand and organize their daily experiences. Concepts such as time (now/before/after), space (in/out), size (big/little), quantity (more/all gone), matching (same/not the same), and categorization emerge during the toddler years.

Skills in symbolic representation emerge first in the recognition of a child's own mirror image. That symbolic understanding is followed by the ability to identify the child's own photograph, and then by skill in pointing to photographs of familiar family and friends. Over time, toddlers are able to understand that two-dimensional drawings represent three-dimensional objects and that both can be identified through another symbol system—words.

How is technology learned during toddlerhood?

Adults are important to toddlers, and what they do represents the gold standard for toddlers. Most adult activities are inherently desirable to the toddler, who indicates through actions or words the desire to "Me do it, too!" They learn a great deal through imitation and experimentation. Toddlers who see adults using cell phones, television remote controls, digital cameras, and computers become as comfortable with these tools as with more conventional devices.

How is technology use facilitated during toddlerhood?

Adults who incorporate technology and various digital images into home and school activities teach toddlers through modeling. Whether referring to family photographs hung on the wall, pointing to the baby's picture that is being used as a screen saver on the computer, or taking a picture on the cell phone while out shopping, they introduce important two-dimensional pictures to toddlers, who eventually learn that those pictures are representations of important people and things in their lives. Because toddlers are so egocentric, images that feature them using the things that interest them are most desirable. Exposure is the key. It is evident that a preschooler on the playground steering a riding toy with one hand while talking on a plastic cell with the other was exposed to the digital world during the toddler years and has naturally incorporated technology into her play and learning.

PICTURE-OBJECT MATCH

Skill

Toddler activities: symbolic representation

Objectives

1. To match objects to their pictures

2. To develop symbolic representational skills

3. To point to named pictures

4. To name pictured objects

Description

Take pictures of toys or common objects that the children see and use daily. Size so the photograph is approximately the actual size of the object, mount on construction paper or poster board, and laminate.

Display the objects and name one, asking one child at a time to give it to you. Repeat with the names of other objects to assess children's ability to recognize the vocabulary. Show each child a picture and ask if the child knows what it is called; if not, say the word.

Lay the photographs out on the tabletop facing the toddler. Hold up one of the objects and ask the child to put it on top of the picture. If the child has difficulty, move the object near each picture, comparing the object and picture until there is a match. Use the words "same" / "not the same" while the pairs are being compared. Once the child understands the idea of "not the same," introduce the word "different."

Extensions

Small-Group Activities

Play the matching game with two toddlers, helping them to learn to take turns while exploring symbolic representation. This game can be played as part of snack time by first taking and printing pictures of the foods to be served. Show the children how to match the pieces of fruit, for example, to their pictures as they are named. Once all of the food items have been matched, have the children help to wash the fruits and watch as they are cut and served.

Independent Explorations

Once the child understands how the game is played, place the pictures and objects in a shallow box on the shelf for selection during free playtime.

One-on-One Instruction

To enhance the toddler's receptive vocabulary, change the picture-object pairs frequently. Introduce the new materials during individual instruction time so the adult can introduce the vocabulary and to be sure that the child is able to make the symbolic matches appropriately. Objects that reflect a theme or areas of interest being explored in the classroom are appropriate for this type of toddler activity.

Family Involvement

During conferences or informal meetings at drop-off or pickup time, show the family how to use this type of matching activity. Talk briefly about why it is important and how parents can make their own materials at home from magazine or catalog pictures of objects they have at home. For example, an advertisement for the child's favorite cereal could be cut from the newspaper. During breakfast, the parent could show the picture and match it to the actual cereal box.

PHOTO LOTTO

Skill

Toddler activities: symbolic representation

Objectives

1. To match like pictures

2. To recognize the names of pictured objects

3. To name pictured objects

4. To increase the understanding of the functional use of objects

Description

Divide a sheet of construction paper into four quadrants. Mount four photographs of common objects, one per square. Make a second set of the same photographs mounted on individual cards of the same size. Laminate the board and the individual cards. Show the children how to mix up the cards, choose one, and identify it. Then look at the pictures on the board and put the card on top of the corresponding photograph on the playing board. Repeat until all the cards have been matched.

Extensions

Small-Group Activities

Make additional sets of cards, mounted on different-colored construction paper, with individual cards made from the same color. Give each child a lotto board of a different color. Sort the individual cards from each set so that all of one type are together. Show the first card, asking the children to look at their boards and to find the matching picture. Give out all of the cards for that object so that each child is able to match a card to his or her colored lotto board. Repeat until all of the photographs have been identified and matched.

Independent Explorations

When a child has mastered a set of matching picture cards, put the materials out for selection as a job during free play.

One-on-One Instruction

Introduce the concept of categories by making lotto sets that belong to a specific group. For example, sets might represent things we eat with, things we use at bath time, animals, clothing, food, or vehicles. Help the child to see the functional relationships between the objects.

Family Involvement

Make an additional set of picture cards and a lotto board to send home. Provide parents with instructions on how to play and why this is a useful skill for toddlers to master. Stress with parents the opportunity to engage the child in a language activity.

Encourage parents to send pictures or illustrations depicting objects or activities that are currently of particular interest to the child to be used to make matching task cards.

COLOR MATCHING GAME

Skill

Toddler activities: matching, sorting, and one-to-one correspondence

Objectives

1. To match a colored object to its colored card

2. To sort objects by color

Description

Find small, inexpensive toys that come in a variety of colors, such as a set of plastic frogs. Scan a photograph or illustration of an object, such as a lily pad, that relates in some way to the toy. Import the illustration into a page layout program, add the color word and print on paper of that color, then laminate. Lay two of the color cards on the table. Hold up one of the toys and show the child how to match the object by color to card of that color. (Say, *Yellow frog. Jump to the yellow lily pad. Jump frog, jump.*) Repeat until all of the toys have been matched to their corresponding color card. To make the task more difficult, add additional color cards and toys.

Extensions

Small-Group Activities

When students in the group are able to match several color sets, put out all of the color cards and mix the objects into a bowl. Ask each child in turn to reach into the bowl to select a toy, look at it, and match it to the correct color card. Name the color as the child makes the match. Have children take turns until all of the objects have been matched. As the children practice, encourage them to name the colors.

Independent Explorations

Tape two color cards to a tray and place the small toys representing those colors in a small bowl. Put the tray on the shelf for a free play choice.

One-on-One Instruction

When introducing a new color to the game, show the color card and have the child search for other objects in the room that are that color. Say the color name each time a new object is found. Take a picture of the color collection, print it, and have the child watch as you write the word. Put it in an individual color booklet for each child, adding other pictures of color collections over time.

Family Involvement

Let the families know that a focus at school for that week will be color matching. For example, parents can challenge their child to help to put away toys by color. (*Let's find all of the red ones first.*)

Ask families to send common objects from home in a designated color to be used for a few days in classroom color-matching activities.

HAPPY, SAD, MAD POSTERS

Skill

Toddler activities: symbolic representation and emotional development

Objectives

1. To recognize one's own emotional state in a mirror
2. To recognize one's own emotional states in photographs
3. To identify various facial expressions in pictures
4. To match and sort pictures of various emotional states
5. To label various emotional states

Description

Play a mirror game with children, making different facial expressions and having them imitate those expressions in the mirror. Name the emotion that goes with that facial expression. (*That's a happy face!*)

Take pictures of children depicting different emotional states to create feeling books for each child. Use the photographs to talk about how to use words to express feelings rather than responding to situations with physical aggression.

Extensions

Small-Group Activities

Print one photograph of each child in the group that depicts a different emotional state. Glue each photograph to a poster. Show the posters one at a time to the group, asking the children to name the emotion. Write the feeling word on the poster. Then, have the children look through old magazines or advertisements to find photographs of other people exhibiting that emotion. Have the children tear or cut out the pictures and glue them on to the emotion poster.

Independent Explorations

Make pairs of emotion cards. Show the toddler how to lay out the cards face up on the table and then match them. Help him until he can do it by himself.

happy

One-on-One Instruction

Sit with the child in front of a mirror. Demonstrate a facial expression that represents an emotional state (joy, fear, anger, surprise). Encourage the child to imitate your facial expressions. Show the child how to look into the mirror to see both reflections. Take a photograph of the child demonstrating the different emotional states, print it, and talk with the child about the name of that emotion.

Family Involvement

Send home the child's feeling book and encourage families to talk about the emotions depicted. Provide information on how to play the mirror imitation game with the child at home.

Encourage parents to send candid photographs of their child expressing various emotions to use in classroom discussions.

❧

MY FIRST NUMBERS

Skill

Toddler activities: beginning math

Objectives

1. To match objects to their photographs

2. To count rational numbers (one and two objects)

3. To match numbers to their numerals

4. To develop one-to-one correspondence

Description

Create a snack center as one of the free play choices. Use two 8- to 12-inch square containers with lids. Place two different snack choices in the containers. Cut cards to fit onto the lids. Decide how many pieces of each type of snack that the children will be able to select for a snack. Take a picture of each type of food, print several small pictures for each food type, and glue the designated number of photographs onto each card. Write that numeral on the cards; laminate the cards and tape each photograph to the corresponding lid. Use the photo cue cards to designate the number of snack items each child may select. The children place one snack item on each pictured food (and later use a designated symbol such as a dot) to ensure that they take the number of snack items designated by the numeral. Once selected, help the children to transfer their food from the picture card to individual plates.

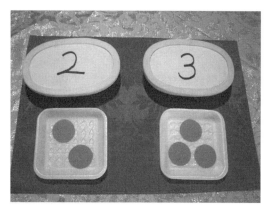

Extensions

Small-Group Activities

Help the children work in pairs to select the correct number of snack items from each container. When finished with snack, talk with the children about what they ate and the number of each type of snack items, referring to the numerals. Then discuss what should be served for snack in future days and have the children help prepare the photo cards. As children become more skillful, substitute circles or other symbols to represent the number of items to be taken.

Independent Explorations

Make a free choice job using the number-snack format, but using wood or plastic fruits and vegetables. The toy fruits that come in pieces, such as sections of oranges, are particularly useful for these tasks. Create the photo cards and put the materials on a tray for the child to choose during free play. He can pretend to set up his tray for snack in the housekeeping center, or make a snack tray for a friend.

One-on-One Instruction

Show the child how to place one of each type of snack on top of its photograph. For example, she might be able to select two pieces of apple and one square of cheese. Point to the numeral for each type of snack and say the number word. Demonstrate how to transfer her snack selections to individual trays to take to the table. Repeat daily during snack time, stressing the same numerals until the child can recognize that number word, the quantity each number word represents, and its corresponding numeral. Then add additional numbers, with smaller snack pieces.

Family Involvement

Suggest to the family that they help their toddler begin to understand quantity and the concept of one-to-one correspondence by making snack mats. They will first draw a box on a sheet of paper for each snack item the child may eat. Then they'll demonstrate how to put one piece of food into each box before eating the snack.

LOOK WHAT I CAN DO!

Skill

Toddler activities: early literacy

Objectives

1. To recognize one's photograph

2. To identify actions in photographs

3. To name actions in photographs

4. To expand vocabulary

Description

Take photographs of the toddlers engaged in a variety of everyday activities. Size them so the pictures will fit into an inexpensive mini photo album, which commonly comes with 4 x 6-inch plastic sleeves. Title each book "Look What I Can Do!". Look at the books with the children, talking about what they were doing in each picture.

Extensions

Small-Group Activities

Make a "Look What I Can Do" book for each child in the group. Sit with the children so they can all see the pictures in one of the books. Open the book randomly so that two pictures are visible. Ask the children to point to a named action. For example, *Show me the picture of Jose pushing. Right, he's pushing the grocery cart to the kitchen. Where's the picture of Jose swinging?*

Independent Explorations

Place the individual "Look What I Can Do!" books in the library for children to view during free play.

One-on-One Instruction

Take random photographs of the children engaged in actions that are not yet represented in their individual "Look What I Can Do!" books. Show the child the photographs on the camera display and have him watch as you quickly transfer them to the computer to download. When appropriate, add a printed title to each picture ("Pushing," "Swinging"). Print, cut out, and add the pictures to the book. Talk with the child about what is represented in the picture.

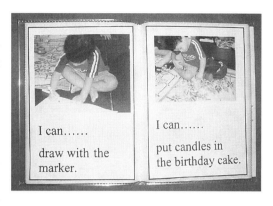

Family Involvement

Periodically send home each child's "Look What I Can Do" book for the child to share with parents or make a second copy so the family can practice new vocabulary words with the child.

PHOTO NAME CARDS

Skill

Toddler activities: early literacy (recognition of photographic images)

Objectives

1. To recognize oneself in a photograph

2. To demonstrate awareness that print has meaning

3. To identify one's own name in print

4. To match one's photograph with a printed name card

Description

Early in the process of symbolic representation, young children respond to their own images in the mirror. After they have made that cognitive leap, they begin to understand that their image can be represented in a photograph.

Take a picture of each child, insert it into a word processing or a page layout program, and add the child's name in print below the photograph. Print the page in color and insert it into a page protector; laminate it or cover it with clear contact paper to protect it and to make it possible to clean as needed.

Show the children their photo pages and watch for a reaction. If a child smiles, looks intently at the picture, or points to indicate recognition, acknowledge the connection by stating that it is indeed a photograph of the child. Point to the picture while saying the child's name and then let your finger drift to the print. Say, *Here's your name. That says Maria.*

Place the photo card in a place where the child will see it many times throughout the day. The place the child is to store his belongings is a natural place to display the photo name card. Each time the child goes to his cubbyhole, say his name as you point to his picture and his printed name.

Extensions

Small-Group Activities

Play "Name That Child" with a small group of children. Pull out a stack of photo name cards for children in the class. Tell the children that you are going to play a guessing game in which their job is to guess which child will be in the picture. Hold up one photograph and have the children identify it. Point to the child's photograph and then to the printed name.

When the children are able to identify each child's photograph, make the game more difficult by describing the child before showing the picture card. For example, *Who has long, black hair?* When the children make their guess(es), verify by showing the photograph.

Independent Explorations

Make a photo card of each of child and teacher in the toddler group or class. Place each into a sheet protector and put it into a small binder. Place the class picture book in the library with other picture books so children can look at the photos and begin to make the connection between the printed word and children's images.

One-on-One Instruction

When older twos can easily match photographs, introduce the idea of print. Use the child's digital image to make a set of two-part reading cards. Place the photograph on the top of the page and type the child's name in large letters with a space between each one. Print two copies of this page, and laminate both of them. Cut the word from the photograph to make two cards from one of the sheets. Show the child how to match his picture to the photograph on the second sheet. Then, show him how to take the card with his printed name on it and match it to the print on the sheet. When the child understands the process, make photo cards of friends or family members so he has more cards to match.

When the child is able to match his name cards, cut the individual letters apart and show him how he can form his printed name by matching the letter card to his photo card.

Family Involvement

Suggest to the family that they take and share family photographs with their children. Send a copy of the class photo book home with different children over the course of several days with a request for the child to point to and name different children in the class. Encourage the parent to use the photographs as the basis for conversation to encourage both receptive and expressive language.

WHAT DO YOU SEE?

Skill

Toddler activities: language and emergent reading

Objectives

1. To identify objects

2. To name objects

3. To imitate a word or words

4. To understand that photographs represent real objects

5. To fill in a missing word appropriately

6. To describe the characteristics (size, color, texture, etc.) and function of objects

Description

Read the picture book *Brown Bear, Brown Bear What Do You See?* by Bill Martin Jr. and illustrated by Eric Carle, to the group. Use the same rhythm from the story to play an I-Spy game. Encourage each child in turn to point an object in the room in the appropriate place in the sentence. For example, say, *Kalani, Kalani, what do you see? I see a* _____ [teddy bear], *here with me.*

Take photographs of the items that the children identified, using them to make a teacher-made book, and call it the "What Do You See?" book. On the left-hand side of each page, write the first sentence. On the right-hand side, insert a photograph and the second sentence with the appropriate word named.

Extensions

Small-Group Activities

Use this activity frequently in small groups to identify different objects as a foundation for other small booklets. Talk about the name, function, and characteristics of

the featured objects. Over time, encourage the children to repeat first the key word and then a phrase and finally the whole sentence.

Independent Explorations

During quiet times of the day, such as just before nap, children may select their own "What Do You See?" books to look at independently.

One-on-One Instruction

Look at one of the "What Do You See?" books with each child. Emphasize an aspect of language development on which each child needs additional practice. One child, for example, may be developing receptive language while another is practicing naming or describing familiar objects.

Family Involvement

Encourage families to play the What Do You See? game during lulls in the day. For example, if the parent has to wait in the car with this child while picking up a sibling, stand in line at the grocery store, or wait in the examination room at the doctor's office, the parent can encourage the child to look around and point to or name interesting objects in the environment. Using the rhyme provides a structure for keeping the game going for a few minutes.

MY FAMILY POSTER

Skill

Toddler activities: language and symbolic representation

Objectives

1. To recognize members of the family
2. To name pictured members of the family
3. To point to or describe family activities

Description

Provide the basic materials and encourage each family to make a poster from photographs of family members and activities. Parents can label the photographs and decorate the poster with the child as they desire. When the family brings in the poster, share it with the children and put it up in the room.

Extensions

Small-Group Activities

Have two or three toddlers look at one poster. Ask questions that will draw on their common experience. Say, *Where's the picture of the dog? What are these people doing?* (eating dinner). *What is Jenny doing there?* (taking a nap).

Independent Explorations

Post the poster at child level so the child can look at it throughout the day. Some young children use the pictures as a way to "check in" emotionally with family and the familiarity of home life while at school.

One-on-One Instruction

Use the family poster as the source of conversation, encouraging the child to name family members and talk about what is happening in each photograph.

Family Involvement

Ask a family member to join the group for a short time on the day parents drop off the family poster. Have the parent and child show their new poster to a few children or the whole group, describing what is happening in each picture.

ROOM SORT

Skill

Toddler activities: memory, categorization, and language

Objectives

1. To identify photographs of common objects

2. To name common objects in photographs

3. To demonstrate understanding of the functional use of common objects

4. To associate common objects with location

5. To sort common objects using only one criterion

Description

Children will look at a photo of an object, identify it, and talk about objects they use at home or school/play group daily. Then they will sort the photographs of those objects by the locations in which they use those objects most often.

Extensions

Small-Group Activities

Show two or three toddlers pictures of objects they use at school or in the toddler group. Ask them to identify what the object is or point to an object when described by function. For example, say, *Which one do we draw with? Crayon.* Once each of the pictures has been discussed, talk about where the class uses those items. Have the children paste those pictures on construction paper for a given location. For example, glue all of the pictures of water table toys on the page for the water play table and the plastic foods on the page for the dramatic play kitchen.

Independent Explorations

Make a series of little booklets of items that belong together in one location and put those in the library for independent perusal.

One-on-One Instruction

During individual conversations, talk about the objects in the set of picture cards. Ask the child to name the object in each picture, and then talk about its function and where it is usually used. Gradually introduce new objects to expand the child's vocabulary and conceptual base.

Family Involvement

Encourage families to help children learn about common objects by using them under supervision and then putting them away in their proper place. For example, towels can be folded and put into the linen closet, and silverware can be sorted into a kitchen tray. Encourage parents to name each item and talk about how to use it.

TODDLERS AND TECHNOLOGY CHECKLIST

	Baseline	Period 1	Period 2
Child: _____	_/_/_	_/_/_	_/_/_

Mechanical Devices

To explore toys with moving parts
To show an interest in mechanical toys
To activate a variety of mechanical toys (depressing buttons, pushing levers, moving knobs, etc.)
To activate one or more mechanical devices (TV remote, light switch, vacuum cleaner on-off switch, etc.)

Imitation

To watch and then imitate simple motor patterns of another person (hold a toy phone with one hand and push the buttons with the index finger of the other hand)
To watch and then imitate the complex motor patterns (three or more steps) of another person (flip up a cell phone, push the buttons, hold it to the ear, talk, push the button to end the call)
To imitate one- to three-word phrases (push the button)

Problem Solving

To experiment with toys and new devices through trial and error
To demonstrate an awareness of cause-and-effect thinking by repeating an action to get the same desired result (twist a knob to make a character pop up on a busy box)
To indicate the ability to plan before using a new toy or device (turn the object to find the functional size or the button to activate a toy)
To demonstrate an awareness of a toy that is not working or is broken
To hand a toy that is not working or that is broken to an adult for assistance (a type of means-end problem solving)

Symbolic Representation

To identify one's own image in a mirror
To identify one's own image in a photograph
To identify the photograph(s) of familiar family and friends
To match objects to photographs
To match objects to illustrations
To identify photographs of familiar items in books when named
To identify illustrations of familiar items in books when named
To match like photographs (lotto-like game)
To match like illustrations (lotto-like game)

12

Children With Special Needs

CHILDREN WITH SPECIAL NEEDS INTRODUCTION

What is a special need?

There are two types of young children with special needs: those who have been identified and those who have yet to be identified. All teachers of young children have, at one time or another, worked with a child with special needs. Because the identification or diagnosis of many developmental delays, disorders, and disabilities is difficult in the very young, teachers and care providers often have children they see struggling with one or more aspects of their development but who are not identified as a child with special needs. Many of those children will be referred for evaluation, and some will be formally identified later as children whose instruction needs to be modified to address their particular learning challenges.

Some young children come into a learning environment, particularly an inclusion setting, with a formal program and specialists to assist the classroom teacher in making needed adaptations. For children who are struggling but who have not yet been evaluated for special needs, the teacher or care provider will need to do as she has always done and experiment with different techniques to help the child learn.

Why is addressing special needs important?

Young children are curious and eager to learn. Those who struggle constantly, are often frustrated, and experience more failure than success often quit trying. Over time, the risks associated with learning far outweigh the rewards, and motivation becomes an issue. Learning for children with special needs is usually harder than for their typically developing peers, and they know that. In order to succeed, they need to believe they can learn and be willing to put in the extra effort that will make achievement possible. By modifying materials, providing additional instruction, encouraging the child, and communicating confidence in that child's ability to learn, the teacher or caregiver is providing the necessary elements for that child to succeed. These early learning experiences form the foundation for later instruction and help the child develop effective student habits that can last a lifetime.

Inclusion of special needs children is an important part of program accreditation and professional certification. A commitment to including children with developmental delays and disabilities in early childhood settings is articulated in the *NAEYC Standards for Early Childhood Professional Preparation* published by the *National Association for the Education of Young Children* (NAEYC[c]). Updated information and resources can be easily accessed from the NAEYC Web site, http://www.naeyc.org, by entering "special needs" in the search option.

How can children with special needs be included?

Every child has something to contribute to the class or the group. Get to know the child, really know him. Talk with those who know the child best to find out about his interests, strengths, and where he may need additional assistance. Explore what techniques work the best, what materials have to be modified, or how the environment can be adapted.

Often, the concern of regular education teachers regarding children with special needs is that these students will "take away" from the other children. While they do need additional attention, particularly in terms of planning, it is important to understand that virtually every technique or course of instruction that is good for the child with special needs is also good for typically developing children. The adaptations that may need to be made for the child with developmental challenges or special needs provide additional practice or another method of instruction for the other children. Additionally, having children with varying abilities and challenges provides typically developing children with a broader range of experiences and perspectives.

How is learning for children with special needs facilitated?

The ideas in this chapter use digital technology to facilitate skills and/or classroom activities that are typical of an early childhood environment. They are time-tested techniques that work with children with special needs, but they can also be used effectively with young or immature children, or children who have not had previous out-of-home care. For example, name-recognition skills needed to put a child's name card on the attendance board are facilitated by including the child's photograph, which can be reduced in size and faded out over time. This is an effective technique for all young learners who are able to recognize their own photographic images but who don't yet recognize letters or words.

There is a very wide range of special needs represented in early childhood special education. The activities in this book target children who might be in inclusion settings with typically developing peers or who are functioning well in self-contained settings. The general concepts and some of the specific activities represented in this chapter can be adapted for lower-functioning children.

This chapter does not include a checklist since the Individualized Education Plan (IEP) is the road map and the document against which progress is measured. This includes a wide range of skills and runs across the entire school curriculum, while the other chapter checklists are domain-specific.

TWO-PART READING CARDS

Skill

Early literacy: recognition of photographic images

Objectives

1. To recognize oneself in a photograph

2. To demonstrate an awareness that print has meaning

3. To identify one's own name in print

4. To match one's photograph with a printed name card

Description

When children are able to point to named pictures, and identify environmental print and symbols, such as recognize their own photographs, Target's bulls-eye logo or the McDonald's golden arches, they may be ready to recognize their own name in print.

A way to gently ease children into this process of word recognition is to make a simple matching puzzle that uses their own pictures and printed name. Take a photograph of each child and insert it into a word processing or a page layout program at the top of the page. Type the child's name in a large font size with a space between each letter and placed below the photograph. Print two copies of the page in color. Cut the name from the photograph on one of the pages to make the puzzle pieces. Laminate all three pieces of the puzzle.

Show the child his puzzle cards. Point to his photograph and then to the word as you say the child's name. Lay the picture on the tabletop and then hand him the puzzle piece of his face. Show the child how to match that piece to the one on the game board. Then pick up the name card, read the child's name aloud, and place it over the word on the game board. Repeat, having the child match both pieces independently.

Extensions

Small-Group Activities

Mix up the picture cards and have each child in the group name the children depicted in the photograph. Lay out a "picture-name" game board for each child in the group. Shuffle the picture pieces and have the children match the pieces to the game boards. Then hold up the printed name card to see if any of the children are able to match the word to one of the game cards. If not, point to the first letter and say the sound. Point to the letters on the game board so the children are able to see how they match. Repeat until each of the cards have been matched.

Independent Explorations

Make a photo card of each of the children and teachers in the class. Put out a group of four to six sets on a tray for a free-choice activity. Note the children who select this activity and monitor to see whether they need any assistance to get started.

One-on-One Instruction

When the child is able to match his name cards, cut the individual letters apart and show him how he can assemble the printed form of his name by matching the letter card to the sequence of letters on his photo card.

As the child becomes skilled at matching his own card and those of other children in the class, take pictures of objects being studied or items of particular interest to the child. Make two-part reading cards for these items to use with this child.

Family Involvement

Make a set of two-part reading cards for the child to take home for additional practice. Encourage the family to make labels with the child's name and tape them to appropriate places around the house to facilitate name recognition and reading skills.

WHAT'S NEXT?

Skill

Mathematics: sequential thinking/temporal awareness

Objectives

1. To demonstrate an understanding of the words "before" and "after"

2. To demonstrate an understanding of "first," "next," and "last"

3. To demonstrate an understanding of "now" and "later"

4. To sequence activity cards in order from the beginning to end

Description

Children with developmental delays or disabilities often have difficulty organizing time and space. Long before they are able to tell time, children can develop a temporal sense by

becoming aware of the sequence of activities. Behavioral upsets can often be avoided when the child is able to understand that what he wants to do will happen after a required activity has occurred. (*We'll feed the goat next. We'll do that right after we have our snack.*)

Take photographs of common activities in the classroom or home care setting. Introduce temporal lessons by making a chart that reads "Before /After" or "Now/Next." Put one of the pictures in the first column and identify it. Then, ask what usually happens after that activity and show the children two task cards as cues. For example, if the first picture shows one of the children eating a snack, the next may show another child putting rubbish into the trash can. Repeat with several activities throughout the school day so the children have practice in understanding the concepts of before-after.

Over time, increase the number of columns on the graphic organizer for first, next, and last. To keep the activity fresh and to help the children generalize these time concepts, feature a different child in the photographs each week.

Extensions

Small-Group Activities

Have one child in the small group select a picture card and put it onto the before-after chart. Encourage him to ask the other children to identify what activity will come next and to put that picture card after his card on the chart.

Independent Explorations

Make a lotto game of the major daily activities. Make a long, linear game board that goes from left to right, with a picture of an activity in each square. Create a set of identical picture cards that are cut into individual squares that the child can match to the photograph on the game board.

One-on-One Instruction

Introduce the idea of an individual itinerary, helping the children to make choices regarding the sequence of activities that they will engage in during the free play time. Explain the choices that will be available and have them put small Velcro-backed picture cards onto their itinerary cards. When a child has completed one task or is wandering aimlessly, refer the child to her task card to see what activity she chose to do next. At the end of the morning or the day, talk with the child briefly about what she did during each of the activities that she chose.

To simplify this activity, make the itinerary card and the individual task cards, but have the child select only one activity at a time. Keep the other cards in an envelope taped to the back of the itinerary.

Family Involvement

Ask parents to use the words *now, next, later, before,* and *after* when the opportunity arises during daily activities at home.

Encourage parents whose children have difficulty with family errands to make a sequence chart using photographs or sketches. This will help the child understand that on this trip, he and mother will have to get gas at the gas station, pick up brother at school, and then get milk at the grocery store. After each activity, the task card is removed from the sequence chart, and a comment is made on what is next. For example, the parent can say, *We've got the gas. Now we have to pick up brother. Then just one stop before we go home.*

PICTURE EXCHANGE

Skill

Language acquisition: communication

Objectives

1. To express wants, needs, and desires nonverbally

2. To engage in meaningful two-way communication

Description

Some children with developmental delays are slow to master expressive language skills, which can lead to frustration and sometimes misbehavior. The picture exchange is a functional method of interaction that helps the child compensate for his or her language delays. In the beginning stages of this nonverbal communication system, take photographs of commonly used objects and items that the child is likely to want. Laminate the photographs for use.

Two adults usually work together with the child during the training phase. One adult entices the child with a desired object, while the second remains behind the child to physically pick up the picture of that item. When the child hands the picture to the first adult, she "exchanges" the picture for the object. Over time, the physical prompts of the second adult are faded out, and the child begins to spontaneously use the picture cards to make requests. Adults can encourage the use of the cards by looking quizzical and asking, *What do you want?* When the child picks up the picture of a ball, respond by saying, *Oh, you want the ball. Here it is.* The goal is for the child to seek out others and to initiate communication using the photographs.

Communication boards for facilitating picture exchange can be simply constructed from poster board by delineating spaces for the photographs to be placed. Laminate the board and the cards. Attach sandpaper or Velcro strips to the cards so

that a corresponding Velcro strip or piece of felt can be affixed to the board .

After the child has developed a mastery of the picture exchange process and regularly uses a large number of picture cards, the teacher can introduce sentence structure. A card for *I want* will be followed by a card for the desired object or action. Other carrier phrases, such as *I see, Where's the* _____, or *Let's*_____ [play] can be added over time. Photographs depicting adjectives and other words that will enhance the child's expressive skills may also be added.

Extensions

Small-Group Activities

Make communication boards to accompany simple games, such as Simon Says. Include photographs of the different body parts the children in the small group are to locate. For example, pat your head, jump, shake your hands, wiggle your fingers.

Independent Explorations

Encourage the children to use those photo cards and communication boards, which they have mastered. Make a matching game using the same pictures for review and reinforcement during center time. These pictures can also be reprinted to create a teacher-made book, such as "Look What I Can Do At School."

One-on-One Instruction

Use one-on-one time to introduce new communication boards or additional vocabulary words. Categories might include words for emotions (how do you feel?), mathematics (big/little, long/short), or art materials (paint, glue sticks, cut with scissors, crayons)

Family Involvement

Family members may want to make simple picture exchange boards to use at home for daily activities. A simple page with numbered boxes could be made, covered with clear contact paper, and then a small piece of Velcro affixed to each box. Then photo cards of the child performing each step of the toileting ritual could be taken, sized to fit into the boxes on the sheet, and then laminated. Talk with the child about what is happening in each picture. (For example, pulling down shorts, pulling down pants, sitting on toilet, using toilet paper, through flushing and hand washing.) Use the picture exchange system to guide the child through the routine.

Other routine boards could be created for setting the table, getting dressed, brushing teeth, or morning routines.

ANTECEDENT-BEHAVIOR-CONSEQUENCE (ABC)

Skill

Behavior management: observing and understanding different types of behavior

Objectives

1. To identify the antecedent(s) of a target behavior and the result of that behavior

2. To talk with the child about what precipitated the behavior

3. To analyze what the child gets out of the behavior as a way of developing alternative strategies

Description

This technique works best when there is one adult designated to take video footage of student interactions, while other adults are free to deal with the children. Capture an episode of behavior, either positive or negative. If a video camera isn't available, a series of photographs from a still camera will suffice.

Analyze the sequence after the event. Sort the scenes or still pictures into three categories. First, identify one target behavior that needs to be addressed. Then, identify the antecedent, or those actions that occurred before the main behavior. For example, if one child bit another (the behavior), look for what was said or done before that encounter. One child might have had a fire truck and the child in question tried to take it from him. They struggled, and the target child bit the child who had the truck. Finally, identify what happened just after the behavior. That information represents the consequence, or the payoff to the child for the behavior. In this example, the teacher may have rushed in to console the child who was bitten, but the target child cradled the fire truck in his arms.

By analyzing the episode, the teachers can develop a strategy for dealing with behavior in a way that has long-term positive results. In the case of the fire truck, the teacher might choose to teach the child how to ask for a toy or go to the teacher for help to get his needs met without hitting or biting. This technique can also be used to promote positive behaviors.

Extensions

Small-Group Activities

Show the picture of the behavior to a small group of children. Have students describe what they see happening in the photograph. Use this opportunity to talk about how each of the children might be feeling, what each wanted to happen, and what each one could have done to get what he or she wanted. The photographs help the child to see, recall, and understand the behaviors that you are referring to as you talk about the incident.

Independent Explorations

Pick three pictures to make a sequencing activity. Make a sequencing board with three medium-sized boxes placed next to each other horizontally. Label the first box "before," the second "during" or "what happened," and the third "after." Have the child sequence the pictures.

For younger or less experienced children, make this a matching game with a photograph in each of the boxes on the sequencing board and use the set of three cards to match to like pictures.

Kamakoa
Jan. 23

Antecedent	Behavior	Consequence
Kamakoa watched Mele, an older child, who was working on a color-matching job.	Kamakoa grabbed the box with the bears and started to pull them off. Mele got upset. The home care provider returned the materials to Mele, telling him he'd have to wait for a turn.	Kamakoa made a sound of protest and then sucked his thumb while he waited for his turn.

Notes:

Kamakoa still has a tendency to grab activities that he finds interesting from the other children, but once corrected, his periods of unhappiness are shorter (1–2 minutes). He has discovered that he can self-regulate his upset by sucking his thumb. We are going to continue to be vigilant in watching his interactions with his peers and helping him to remember to ask, not grab, and that sometimes he needs to wait his turn for materials.

One-on-One Instruction

Once the child has sequenced the photographs used for the independent exploration, have the child describe to an adult the story that she just sequenced. The teacher could then record what the child has said, turning her words into text. This type of instructional dialog helps the child associate appropriate language to the pictured behaviors.

Family Involvement

Share various ABC photo logs with the parents as a foundation for discussion on specific behaviors that can be encouraged or discouraged both at home and at school.

WHAT'S HAPPENING?

Skills

Language: receptive and expressive

Objectives

1. To identify pictured actions
2. To recognize and label verbs
3. To describe in phrases or sentences what is going on in a photograph
4. To sequence a series of actions from beginning to end
5. To enhance memory skills

Description

Much of what young children and older children with special needs do in school can be considered "process" work. Rather than producing a high quality final product, the learning occurs during the process of the activity. Singing songs, pulling and pounding play dough, or watering the seeds of newly planted vegetables are examples of process activities. In these tasks, the child interacts with materials and sometimes other children, but there is no physical evidence of learning after the materials have been put away. By taking random photographs while children are engaged in these process jobs, the teacher can make the experience

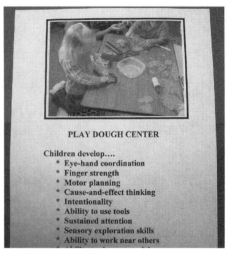

more permanent. The photograph can be used in a variety of ways, all of which serve the purpose of freezing the experience in time so it can be retrieved and discussed.

Extensions

Small-Group Activities

Print and cut out pictures from two or more categories of process play. Have the small group of children talk about each photograph and sort them into the appropriate groupings. Ask the children what to call each group and write that word on a poster. Then have the children glue the photographs onto each poster by category. Add a brief description of what is being learned in the activity to inform parents and volunteers. Laminate the finished product and display in the area in which that activity usually occurs.

Independent Explorations

Hang the posters made in the small-group activity in that area of the room so that children can look at other examples of children in the class playing dress up, completing wooden puzzles, making Lego constructions, or engaged in other process activities.

One-on-One Instruction

Take photographs that depict targeted vocabulary and verbal expressive skills. If the child is working on expanding expressive vocabulary, for example, take pictures of the child using a variety of classroom materials and assemble them. Lay out several picture cards and play a guessing game, having the child find the card that you describe. Ask, *Where's the picture of you cutting with the scissors?*

Family Involvement

Print copies of these process activities either to send home with a brief comment at the end of each day or to collect and send home at the end of the week.

If parents have access to a digital camera or phone, encourage them to send in similar pictures of things the child does at home. Taking a bath, making cookies with Mom, going to soccer to watch an older sibling, or washing the car with Uncle are examples of process activities that might take place at home.

INDIVIDUAL ITINERARIES

Skill

School behaviors: intentionality

Objectives

1. To develop a plan for one's time
2. To implement the plan
3. To review the success of the plan

Description

A common challenge for young children and individuals with special needs is the use of time. To help them learn to organize their time, show them how to create a plan. Develop a sheet with two parts. Label the top as "Plan" and include a place for the date stamp. Have the child look at miniature photographs of possible free play choices of activities. Ask the child what she would like to do first today. Once she's made her selection, show her how to apply the glue stick to the back of that picture and then place it in the first position on the card. Repeat with one, two, or three more selections. Review the child's choices with her and then direct her to the area of her first choice.

Extensions

Small-Group Activities

Encourage children to compare their itineraries to find commonalities. Have each child describe where he or she planned to go during the morning. Ask, *Who chose the art center next? You may go now together.*

Independent Explorations

When the child has finished working or playing in the first area, have her refer to her itinerary, place a check mark by the center she has completed, and then look to see where she should go next.

One-on-One Instruction

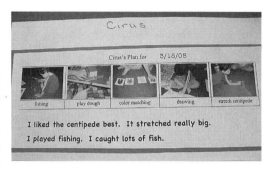

Toward the end of the day, sit down briefly with each child and go over the plan. Help the child to recall what he did and to talk about his activities. Write down his responses and keep each plan in a folder by date.

As the child becomes more skilled at making and using his itinerary, talk with him at the end of the day about how the plan worked. For example, you might inquire as to whether the child finished all of his activities that day or whether in the future he needs to plan for longer times in fewer centers.

Family Involvement

Save each child's itineraries in a folder by date. Make comments on the child's progress in planning and implementing his activities. Share the collection of plans with the parent to note progress in the child's ability to become more self-directed.

NUMBER HUNT

Skill

Mathematics: number-numeral correspondence

Objectives

1. To recognize basic numerals
2. To count rationally
3. To match numbers and numerals
4. To recognize quantities as more/less, greater/fewer

Description

When working on early number (quantity) skills and numeral recognition, have a small group of children do a number hunt. Make photo cards of common objects in the classroom. Be sure there are one to three objects for each photograph in clear sight. Give the pictures to the children and ask them to find these objects.

Once they've found the objects, have the children group them. Ask them to count the number in each grouping (one, two, and three objects). Help children to take a photograph of each of the groupings, stressing the number in each set. Print and cut out the photographs.

Extensions

Small-Group Activities

Place a numeral on the top of a large piece of colored construction paper. Ask the children to go through the pictures that they took, count the objects in the pictures, and then put them into the correct grouping. Write the numeral and name of the objects that go with the picture. Glue onto the construction paper and post in the classroom.

Independent Explorations

Make a box of the objects pictured in the photographs and individual photo cards. Have the child match the object to the picture. For more advanced children, make two photo cards for each object and write a numeral on each card. Laminate the cards to make a number-numeral matching job.

One-on-One Instruction

Help the child to make a "one-two" booklet to take home. Fold several sheets of typing paper in half and staple. Write "My Number Book" on the cover, with the numeral 1 on the left-hand of each page and the numeral 2 on the right-hand side. Ask the child to write her name on the cover. Then have her find pairs of object pictures (paintbrushes, cookie cutters, toy cars, and bubble wands). Once the child has matched the pairs, show her how to glue the picture of one paintbrush on the left side of the page under the numeral 1 and two paintbrushes under the numeral 2 on the right side. Repeat with the other objects.

Family Involvement

Send each child's individual number booklet home as the basis of conversation between parent and child. Encourage the parent to ask what each object is, what it is used for, and how many there are.

SELF-HELP GRAPH

Skill

Personal care: self-help

Objectives

1. To encourage children to master basic self-help skills

2. To introduce the concept of graphing

3. To make one-to-one correspondence

Description

Children with special needs often have self-help skills written into their Individualized Educational Plans (IEPs), and, typically, developing preschoolers are still working to master self-care. One way to document individual children's mastery of critical self-help skills while introducing the mathematical concept of graphing is to create a simple graph for the class. Write each child's name in a column and place a photograph at the bottom of each column. Along the left side of the graph, picture and label important self-help skills. For example, columns might be labeled "Eat with a fork," "Drink from a cup without spilling," "Pour from a small pitcher," "Put on own shoes," "Wash and dry hands."

Hang the poster in a prominent place in the room and refer to it daily. When a child has mastered a new skill, he can color the corresponding box on his column as the other children applaud his achievement.

Extensions

Small-Group Activities

Make a Concentration card game using the self-help photos. Print, laminate, and cut out two pictures of each self-help skill. Show the children how to turn all of the cards facedown on the table. The first player turns over two cards and identifies the pictures. If the pictures match, she can keep the cards and take another turn. If not, she has to return the cards to their original positions facedown and the next player takes a turn. Continue until all of the cards have been matched. Finish the activity by having the children do one of the pictured activities.

Independent Explorations

Once a child is able to consistently demonstrate a specific self-help skill, set up activities with photo instructions so the child is able to do the job independently. For example, once the child is able to pour from a small pitcher, set up a snack center with

Look At Our Self Help Skills!

	Cirus	Dillan	Kamakoa	Kamilia	Zeus
Pour from a small pitcher					
Drink from a small glass				⭐	
Drink from a small cup	⭐	⭐		⭐	
Drink using a straw	⭐	⭐	⭐	⭐	⭐

a pitcher and glass with the snack beverage, and include a photo of a child pouring from the pitcher into the glass.

One-on-One Instruction

Provide step-by-step instruction and a range of materials for those self-help skills that need additional practice. For example, if several children need work on buttoning, make a variety of simple button boards and have clothing items with buttons of various sizes and textures. Start with unbuttoning large buttons through an extra large buttonhole. Help each child practice until he or she has mastered each self-help skill.

Family Involvement

Self-help is an area where parents can provide much needed additional practice. Most of these skills are ones the parents are already helping their children to achieve. Communicate regularly on progress and send home photos of successful techniques or a newly mastered skill. Encourage families to share information on what is working at home.

WHO IS NOT HERE TODAY?

Skill

Personal care: good health habits

Objectives

1. To understand the connection between health habits and illness/wellness

2. To practice good health habits

3. To identify the photographs of class members

4. To understand the concepts of present and absent

Description

Help children understand the difficult connection between their health habits and illness or wellness. Talk about good health habits, such as covering one's mouth with coughing, sneezing into a tissue, frequent hand washing, and not using another's toothbrush. Read storybooks about germs and health and then make a companion chart to use with the attendance chart.

Make a pocket chart labeled "Who Is Not Here" to hold the picture name cards of the children who are absent. Also, make some cards representing the various illnesses that cause young children to miss school.

Once all students present have put their name card on the traditional classroom chart, go through the cards of the children who are absent. Place those cards into the new chart. If there is information from parents about why the child is not present, put up a picture card to represent that reason. For example, if Jennifer is home sick with an earache, put up her card and next to it put up an illustration depicting an earache.

Talk with the children about the importance of hand washing and other basic health habits in avoiding illness.

Extensions

Small-Group Activities

In a small group, talk about common types of illnesses and the children's personal experiences of being sick. Look at a picture book of real germs under high magnification. Then, through artwork, have the children make a representation of what the germs might look like if they could see them. They could make drawings, paintings, collages, or play dough representations of germs.

Independent Explorations

Set up the germ representation artwork in a display and allow the children to walk through the "gallery" to look at how different children imaged the germs.

One-on-One Instruction

Once each child is finished with his art-work, ask the child to tell you about it. Write down what the child says and post that with the art. Then ask the child to describe one technique for avoiding those germs.

Family Involvement

Ask the family to contact the school when they know the child will not be in attendance. Let them know that the class is working on good health habits and that you would like their help in identifying what type of illness the child has when he or she is out sick. That way, you can chart it for the group and encourage them to continue to wash their hands thoroughly, cover their mouths when coughing, and not sneeze on each other. Post a picture of the "Who Is Not Here" chart either on the secure class Internet site or at the sign-out area.

COMMUNICATIONS BOOK

Skill

Language: acquisition and home-school communications

Objectives

1. To inform parents of a child's progress

2. To provide photographs that can serve as a source of conversation between parent and child

Description

Young children and children with disabilities have limited language and memory skills with which to describe their day at school to family members. Communication between home and school is particularly important during the early years. Set up a communication book that can go back and forth from home to school daily. A simple notebook could serve as the log, with a handwritten note each day about the relevant details of what went on in school. A digital photo can be printed and glued into the book to support the text.

Parents are encouraged to respond to the note and to send the log back to school with any information that they think would be useful for the teacher to know.

Extensions

Small-Group Activities

During a small-group activity, take a variety of pictures. Immediately export the photographs to the computer and print as the children watch. Have the children talk about the pictures and record what the children say as captions to the pictures. Place one of the photos into a stand-up picture frame to display by the parent sign-out sheet.

One-on-One Instruction

Show the child two pictures from his school day and ask the child to talk about what he was doing in each one. Have the child choose which picture to include in the communication log that he will take home for his parents. Record any of the child's verbal communications as well.

Family Involvement

Encourage parents to provide important information from home, such as when their child has had a poor night's sleep, had a favorite aunt visiting, or gotten a new puppy. A note about any change in the child's physical condition or home routine that may impact his behavior during the school day is useful for the teacher. Good home-school communication is vital to a successful program for all children, but particularly those with special needs.

References

Bowman, B. (2006). Standards at the heart of educational equity. *Young Children, September 2006*, 42–48.

Center for Research on Education, Diversity & Excellence. "The CREDE Five Standards for Effective Pedagogy and Learning." Retrieved April 17, 2009 from http://crede.berkeley.edu/research/crede/standards.html

Center for Research on Education, Diversity & Excellence. (2002). "A Rubric for Observing Classroom Enactments of CREDE's Standards for Effective Pedagogy." Retrieved April 17, 2009 from http://crede.berkeley.edu/research/tier/spc.html

Entz, S. (2007). Why pedagogy matters: The importance of teaching in a standards-based environment. *Forum on Public Policy*. Retrieved from http://www.forumonpublicpolicy.com/papersspr07

Microsoft Corporation. (1999). *Encarta World English Dictionary*. Bloomsbury Publishing, Plc.

National Association for the Education of Young Children (NAEYC[a]). *Early learning standards: Creating the conditions for success*. A Joint Position Statement of the National Association for the Education of Young Children and the National Association of Early Childhood Specialists in State Departments of Education (NAECS/SDE). Retrieved April 17, 2009 from http://www.journal.naeyc.org

National Association for the Education of Young Children (NAEYC[b]). *Learning to read and write: Developmentally appropriate practices for young children*. A Joint Publication with the International Reading Association (IRA). In *Young Children, 53 (4)*, 30–46. Retrieved April 17, 2009 from http://www.naeyc.org

National Association for the Education of Young Children (NAEYC[c]). (2002). "NAEYC Standards for Early Childhood Professional Preparation." Retrieved March 17, 2009 from http://www.naeyc.org

Parten, M. B. (1932). Social participation among preschool children. *Journal of Abnormal and Social Psychology, 27*, 243–269.

Smiliansky, S. & Shefatya, L. (1990). *Facilitating play: A medium for promoting cognitive, socio-emotional and academic development in young children*. Gaitherburg, Maryland: Psychosocial and Educational Publishing.

Tharp, R. G. & Gallimore, R. (1988). *Rousing minds to life: Teaching, learning and schooling in social context*. New York: Cambridge University Press.

Tharp, R.G., Estrada, P., Dalton, S.S., & Yamauchi, L. (2000). *Teaching transformed: Achieving excellence, fairness, inclusion and harmony*. Boulder, Colorado: Westview.

Index